A divine song purifying the soul

The Stairway to Heaven along the central axis on the south slope has 6,666 steps, an auspicious number to pilgrims making the ascent.

CONTENTS

Chapter I

Towering Mount Taishan

Ancient Myths about Mount Taishan

Among China's ancient myths, one concerns the fairy lady Magu who witnessed the East Sea changing into fertile land three times. Another tells the tales of the Yan Emperor's little daughter who drowned while playing in the East Sea. The girl's spirit lingered on and changed into the mythical bird called Jingwei who tried to fill up the sea with pebbles and twigs she brought from the Western Mountain. She kept on flying between the mountain and the sea until it was finally filled in. Consequently an island in the sea became a mountain on dry land — Mount Taishan — and the creeks that had not yet been filled in became four rivers — the Yellow, Jishui, Wenhe and Sishui rivers, and the remaining puddles became lakes and marshland. On this land created by Jingwei, legend has it that the goddess Nuwa shaped many figures out of clay — the ancestors of the yellow race.

Mythology is just that — mythology. But among all the fantastic imaginings and stirring tales are certain scientific and historical elements.

Painting of the separating of heaven and earth by the mythical creator of the universe Pangu, whose head, after his death, became Mount Taishan.

Ancient Chinese mythology relates that the goddess Nuwa, who made humans out of clay, was the sister and later the wife of Fuxi, the legendary ancestor of the Chinese people. Pictured here are their images as described in Chinese myth. (from *Chinese Myths and Legends*)

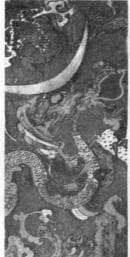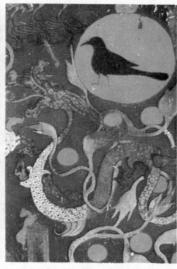

Patchwork of fields in Shandong Province

3

The Yellow River, a golden ribbon in the setting sun, as seen from the summit of Mount Taishan

The Wenhe River running south of Mount Taishan

The Formation of Mount Taishan

This tiny planet we inhabit has been traveling in the universe for over 5 billion years. About 2.5 billion years ago, roughly in its middle age, the earth experienced a tremendous upheaval. From beneath the huge rumbling waves, an immense subsidence zone and a deep ocean trough with thick deposits of silts rose to form a vast landmass with a huge mountain system. For the first time in history, ancient Mount Taishan emerged from the sea.

Isotopic analysis has revealed the granite by the Hushan Reservoir on the mountain's southern slope is 2.68 billion years old, and that by the Zhongtianmen (Mid-way Gate to Heaven) 2.075 billion years. This is very old indeed.

Nearly 2 billion years of erosion and weathering resulted in ancient Mount Taishan having a gentle topography. Then, during the early Paleozoic Era about 600 million years ago, the land in North China began to sink steadily and the mountain was submerged in the sea once again.

On the bank of the Wenhe River that flows below Mount Taishan, people have found rocks with swallow-like relief patterns in them. Locally known as "swallow rocks," they are in fact trilobite fossils, a type of arthropod living in the sea some 600 million years ago.

During the late Mesozoic Era over 100 million years ago, as a result of the compression and under-thrust of the Pacific Plate to the Eurasia Plate and under the influence of the Yanshan Mountains movement in North China, the huge Taiqian fault, stretching 100 kilometers from Laiwu to Tai'an, rose sharply to

Majestic Mount Taishan, known as the mountain of the country

Rocks on Mount Taishan, weathered by wind and rain for over two billion years

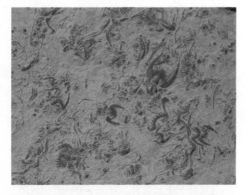

About 600 million years ago, the land in North China began to sink steadily and Mount Taishan was submerged in the sea. Pictured here are fossils of trilobite, a marine creature living of the time.

The great mountain emerging form the sea of clouds

form a tilted fault-block mountain sloping from south to north. The 2,000-meter-thick sedimentary layer brought up from the seabed was eroded and denuded during the rise, and the ancient rocks on Mount Taishan were brought to light once

again. The granites, affected by the metamorphism, being highly resistant to weathering, formed the mountain's rugged crags and precipitous cliffs.

The bulging process was long drawn out, lasting until about 30 million years ago when, on the eastern Eurasian landmass, on the western Pacific rim, Mount Taishan emerged — lofty and mighty, towering heavenward.

Moon Viewing Peak in the sunset glow

Looking west from the summit toward golden clouds after rain

The Taiqian fault behind the Mid-way Gate to Heaven

Oblique view of the Lu Viewing Terrace

Lu Viewing Terrace on the top of Mount Taishan

The Status of Mount Taishan

Jade Emperor Summit, the main peak of Mount Taishan, is 1,545 meters above sea level. In terms of altitude Mount Taishan can hardly claim pride of place in China; let alone comparisons with Qomolangma (Mount Everest), Mount sands of years, Mount Taishan has held the supreme position among the five sacred mountains — all of China's mountains even. Furthermore, inscriptions on its cliffs use such laudatory descriptions as "towering majesty in the east," "supporting the sky and holding up the sun" and "as lofty as heaven." So, what is the

The city of Tai'an, at the foot of Mount Taishan, is 153 meters above sea level; while the main peak, the Jade Emperor Summit, stands at 1,545 meters above sea level.

Taishan is only the 16th highest mountain in China, and of the five sacred mountains, it is only the third highest — being only half high of Mount Wutai in Shanxi Province. Nonetheless, for thousands of years, Mount Taishan has held reason for this?

Enlarged land satellite images show that Mount Taishan is the highest mountain around within a several-hundred-kilometer radius.

"Most Revered of the Five Sacred Mountains," inscribed on the front face of the Jade Emperor Summit

The name "Mount Taishan" was first used in an poem in the ancient *Book of Songs · Eulogy for the State of Lu,* written in praise of the king of Lu's victories: "Mount Taishan is so majestic that all the people of Lu can see it clearly if they raise their heads." Between the 11th and 3rd century BC, Shan-dong Province, in which Mount Taishan is situated, was a fiefdom of the kingdoms of Lu and Qi. This is why today Shandong is called "Lu" for short, alternatively "the land of Qi and Lu."

As the word "tai" means "large, unobstructed and peaceful," the name "Taishan" can mean the largest of mountains, a mountain touching the heavens, and mountain of stability.

Another of its names is Daizong, a term used in the classics of the Warring States Period (475-221 BC). "Dai" means "large mountain," and "zong" means "the eldest," the combination meaning "the eldest of large mountains."

In absolute terms Mount Taishan can-

On the vast land between the Yanshan and Taihang mountains in the north, the Yangtze River in the south, between Mount Huashan and Mount Funiu in the west and the ocean in the east, Mount Taishan stands majestic and fully deserving the honor of oldest of all mountains. So, since antiquity it has been called "Taishan (Greatest Mountain)" or "Daizong (The Oldest of Large Mountains)."

not be considered the highest of China's mountains, but because it is close to the sea and rises abruptly from the relatively low rolling hills and plains of Qi and Lu, its relative height is quite impressive. Within the nine kilometers between Taicheng, former seat of Tai'an municipal government, and the top of the mountain, is an altitude difference of 1,395 meters. Ravines and ledges are a feature of the relief. Three big faults on the southern slope — Yunbuqiao, Midway Gate to Heaven and Taiqian — form three steep tiers with big height differentials: the Mid-way Gate to Heaven is nearly 700 meters higher than Taicheng and the Yuhuang Summit is nearly 700 meters higher than the Mid-way Gate to Heaven. The drop from and beyond the height of the Mid-way Gate to Heaven is 500 to 800 meters deep, creating awe-inspiring precipitous cliffs and

"Number One Mountain on Earth," inscribed on the west side of the Jade Emperor Summit

Icy cliffs soaring above the Cloud Step Bridge fault

deep ravines.

The majesty of Mount Taishan has profoundly moved many visitors of every age — emperors who took themselves as the son of heaven, proud high-ranking officials, brilliant poets, and ordinary people too.

Some 2,000 years ago when Emperor Wu of the Western Han Dynasty (206 BC-24 AD), famed for his great talent and bold vision, toured the mountain, he was overwhelmed by its heroic presence and in one breath expressed eight reactions: "Towering! Majestic! Great! Marvelous! Grand! Glorious! Startling! Incredible!"

"Standing Tall in the East," inscribed on the east side of the Jade Emperor Summit

"Rising Abruptly from Earth and Reaching the Sky," inscribed on the west side of the Sun Viewing Peak

15

Ascending Mount Taishan — A Great Life Experience

Mount Taishan has been praised as one of "earth's great sights" and as one of the "world's wonders" since ancient times. It is rich in terms of history, appearance, spiritual and cultural significance. There is an ancient saying that "No mountain is larger than Mount Taishan and no history is longer than that of Mount Taishan." The magnificent massif, its towering appearance, the lofty spirit it represents, the brilliant culture it embodies, and its long history, have com-

bined to make Mount Taishan the spiritual support of feudal emperors and an embodiment of the Chinese people in the eyes of scholars, poets, persons of ideals and integrity and common folk alike. In particular, ascending Mount Taishan was thought auspicious by the literati and poets, or those roaming the empire with books and swords, those wandering through Qi and Lu after problems in their official careers, those passing through because of the vicissitudes of life, and those living the vagabond life, who invariably always thought it worthwhile to roam on and communicate with the huge

Archway, north of the First Gate to Heaven, built in 1560 to commemorate the visit of Confucius. The inscription above the archway indicates this was where Confucius stopped, and the side steles say "Number One Mountain" (on the left) and "You must start here to scale the heights."(on the right)

mountain. And Mount Taishan did always inspire their spirits to be "as lofty as heaven," which were given full expression in poetry and prose that emerged as they ascended.

The section above the South Gate to Heaven was deemed a fairy land where monarchs communed with the gods.

The thinker Mencius (372-289 BC) wrote "When Confucius ascended Mount Taishan the world seemed to dwindle." Confucius (551-479 BC) was an earlier Chinese thinker and educator and though the two lived in different ages, their teachings and ideas came down in one continuous line. When Confucius climbed the mountain and overlooked the world below, he felt his vision expanded and ambition spurred on. Many who came later to the summit of Mount Taishan shared similar feelings.

In late spring of 742, Li Bai, the great romantic poet of the Tang Dynasty (618-907), followed the same route that the Tang Emperor Xuanzong (r. 712-756) had taken when paying homage to the mountain, and ascended the summit. Standing at the South Gate to Heaven and pushing aside the clouds, the poet could not help but cry out,

"Looking up and down at the Landscape," inscribed on the east of the Jade Emperor Summit

"My spirit glows with pride and happiness, as if between heaven and earth!" In the caressing breeze, Li Bai suddenly felt his mind purified, even the universe seemed to shrink, and he sang out loud: "The vast universe is indeed small. What should I care if I now pass away."

While Confucius' ascent of Taishan made the empire seem to dwindle and encouraged the sage to concern himself with the affairs of all of China rather than just the limited world of Qi and Lu, Li Bai's ascent and his reaction to the dwarfed universe below him made the poet forsake the meaningless hubbub of this mortal world to seek spiritual freedom and independence of character.

The Yuan Dynasty (1271-1368) man of letters Zhang Yanghao also left a poem entitled *Climbing Mount Taishan*, "To heaven the wind and cloud rise high, what

delight to have seen such a spectacle in my life," expressing the sentiment of all who have been to the mountain.

Indeed, viewing the scenery as you ascend Mount Taishan is one of life's great delights. As one poem puts it, "The mists rising in the vision, the vast landscape unfurling like a scroll," it seems that all of China is like a huge map spread out flat before your eyes. Standing on top of the mountain, watching the floating clouds disappear on the sea in the east, listening to the wind and rain from the Central Plains in the west, and reflecting on the tremendous changes of history, you can hardly help songs and poetry springing to your lips, feeling purified and expansive; are there any frustrations that cannot be overcome, any gloom that cannot be dispelled?

Plaque at the Heaven and Earth Square, with relief carving of Confucius's visit to Mount Taishan and Mencius' words: "Ascending Mount Taishan, the world seemed to dwindle."

Sea of Clouds on Mount Taishan

"Aspiring to dwarf the world, I come to climb Mount Taishan. Looking up at the summit, only white clouds linger."

Mount Taishan's cloud seas are really a wondrous spectacle. Back in the Warring States Period, people were already saying that all the clouds on earth originated from Mount Taishan. A certain Gongyang Gao held that when the mountain quickly sinks into gloom. Standing at the summit, you see dark clouds looming over, hear thunder rolling below, making you feel as if you were re-experiencing scenes of remote antiquity when Mount Taishan first emerged and rumbled from below the sea. Clouds, like eruptions from deep within the earth, swiftly engulf peaks and cliffs, and flood down the slopes like glaciers of ancient times. After a while, wind and rain both cease, a vast sea of

Surging clouds over Wangfu Mountain as seen westward from Mount Taishan

Taishan's clouds and mists met the rocky cliffs they would rise, mass together as huge patches of cloud, and spread everywhere in no time at all.

When the mountain wind blows up, the sky fills with clouds and mists and clouds spreads below your feet, transforming peaks into isolated fairly islets. Overwhelmed by such marvelous scenes, your thoughts and feelings surge along with the "sea of clouds."

Cascading clouds, rolling down the mountainside

High cirrus cloud streaks the sky.

The summit of Mount Taishan seems to be a bobbing
boat in the sea of clouds.

Mists curling up the slopes from the deep valleys

Watching Sunrise on Mount Taishan

As people moved west to China's Central Plains and to the upper and middle reaches of the Yellow River from coastal regions and areas around Mount Taishan, they came to see Mount Taishan as the great mountain of the east, that the east was where the sun originated, that the sun brought with it light and warmth, dispelling darkness and cold. Wherever there was light and warmth, life would exist and the land would be green. So, the ancestors called the first God of Mount Taishan "Taihao" (Sun God). Thus Mount Taishan can be seen as the first ancestor mountain of the Chinese people.

The sun is the universe's largest and most brilliant object visible to the naked

At the dawn of a new day, the sun begins to emerge.

The rising sun

The sun has risen.

Sunrise seen at the Rear Rock Basin

eye. The splendid sight of the red sun rising in the east best gives people enthusiasm, hope and longing for goodliness. Watching the sunrise from the Sun Viewing Peak on Mount Taishan has been a marvelous spectacle in every age, and is indeed one of the "greatest sights of the earth."

For centuries, watching sunrise from Mount Taishan has been seen by the Chinese as a valuable life experience. To make sure you do not miss the most gorgeous spectacle on earth, you have to reach the top before dawn. Many climb the mountain and sleep on the Heavenly Street the night before so as to be perfectly sure.

As for the best time to watch the sunrise, three occasions were recommended by people of the Yuan Dynasty: during the first month of the Chinese lunar calendar on mornings without rain and no mists on the sea; late autumn on mornings refreshed and dust-free after rain; or mid-winter on cloud and mist-free mornings after snow. In other words, only in the cool late autumn and severe winter with little cloud and mist will the red sun reveal its grandeur to repay those who have climbed the mountain in the bitter cold and waited with great patience through the long darkness.

Sunrises can be seen from many mountains, but the view from the top of Mount Taishan is incomparable. When the sun first appears, it ducks behind the clouds, half in, half out. As the orb slowly rises, it seems to bob between the crests and troughs of the surging waves, a flickering, uncertain light. For a moment, you can see a miraculous pair of twin suns: one in the air and the other a reflection on the glittering sea.

In the east, where sea meets sky, the dawn rays turn gray to pale yellow, then to orange red as rosy clouds suffuse and brighten the whole sky. Then suddenly, the Sun God rides its dazzling carriage, rushing from deep within the boiling cloud sea, pushing aside the shawl of flaming beams and ascending slowly with a corona of fiery sunrays. Soon, golden rays like burning torches light up the peaks. The sun that brings warmth and life to man now casts its limitless light and heat over the wakening land of China.

Asia, where the sun rises, greets a magnificent new day.

Chapter II

Mount Taishan, the Country's Watch Guard

Mysterious Symbols

On the mountaintop, huge flames rise high in the air, licking at the rising sun. What an impressive scene, what a religious fervor! Some 4,500 years ago, the tribes living near Mount Taishan would burn bonfires on the mountain, offering sacrifices to the great Sun God, the supreme dictator of the universe and all living things. This sacred religious ceremony was simplified into a mysterious symbol, inscribed on pottery sacrificial vessels and colored red. By doing so, a stirring moment in history was permanently recorded.

This pottery mark ⚞ has been found time after time in the Zhucheng ruins in Lingyanghe, Juxian County, which belongs to the Dawenkou Culture in Shandong. The mysterious but meaningful symbol consists of three parts: the circle on top is agreed to represent the

Seven examples of the 20-odd graphic symbols (referred to as "graphic characters" by archaeologists) engraved on the same sections of the pottery *zuns* excavated at the Dawenkou Culture site at Lingyanghe, Juxian County

sun and the five peaks at the bottom represent mountains, but opinions differ about the shape in the middle: some say that it is a cloud, others a big bird, and still others argue that it is a flame. So what is it then? Let's first look at a mark, ⚞, inscribed on a tortoise shell excavated in Shang Dynasty (16th -11th century BC) ruins in Anyang, Henan Province. This character is 烛 (candlelight), containing a shape △ similar to that found in Juxian, and the shape is placed above the symbol 𝕀𝕀 for vessels to produce the meaning flame. Therefore, it can be concluded that the shape found on the Juxian pottery refers to flame.

The symbol of mountains on the pottery reveals that primitive religion of mountain worship did exist in the coastal and Mount Taishan areas some 5,000 years ago. As the highest mountain in the region, it was quite natural that Mount Taishan should become an object of worship for the people of the New Stone Age.

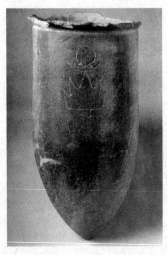

Incised markings on a pottery wine vessel called *zun* (from *History of Relics of Juxian County*)

Culture of Remote Antiquity at Mount Taishan

Commemorative stone memorial erected, in 1982, by the Shandong provincial government to mark the placing of the Dawenkou Culture site under state-level protection

More and more archaeological discoveries show the existence of a "crescent-shaped" arc of ancient Pacific culture along the coast of southeast China, and that Mount Taishan was quite likely the sacred mountain worshipped by people living within the arc.

In the mid-Pleistocene Epoch of the Cenozoic Era some 400,000-500,000 years ago, ape man already roamed about in what is now Shandong, as proved by the fossils of an ancient ape man, named the "Yiyuan Man" after the place where it was discovered — Qizi'an Mountain in Yiyuan County, Linyi. The Yiyuan Man, like Peking Man, was the ancestor of the Chinese people and created the ancient civilization in the region of Shandong.

The ruins of megalithic culture cre-

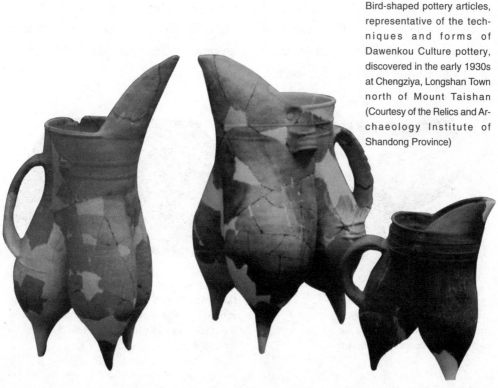

Bird-shaped pottery articles, representative of the techniques and forms of Dawenkou Culture pottery, discovered in the early 1930s at Chengziya, Longshan Town north of Mount Taishan (Courtesy of the Relics and Archaeology Institute of Shandong Province)

ated by primitive people can still be seen at Wangmu Mountain in Zichuan and Yatouji in Rongcheng.

In 1959, the excavation of 133 tombs at Dawenkou at the foot of Mount Taishan ushered in the study of the Dawenkou Culture, a brilliant type of ancient Chinese civilization. This 6,000-year-old New Stone Age culture was in advance of others for more than 1,000 years. The powerful clans, creators of the Dawenkou culture, migrated westward to the north and west of today's Henan Province, penetrating deeply into the dominant culture of the middle reaches of the Yellow River. The people also reached the Yangtze River valley in the south and had their own images and symbols engraved on the jade articles and pottery wine vessels of the Liangzhu Culture that was widespread in areas south of the lower reaches of the Yangtze.

Fuxi, the legendary ancestor of the Chinese people, is believed to have created the Dawenkou Culture, which, along with its derivative Longshan Culture, dominated the lives of the eastern tribal people living in the Mount Taishan region of east China and a major element of the Chinese race at a specific stage of its development.

Archaeologists hold that both the late Neolithic Longshan Culture and the Bronze Age Erlitou Culture in Henan Province were profoundly influenced by the east culture that originated between the coast and Mount Taishan. As the Chinese ancestors pioneered an era of civilization, a corridor of cultural diffusion emerged running in an east-west direction, between the lower reaches of the Yellow River around Mount Taishan and areas along the middle reaches of the Yellow River.

Red pottery *dou* with sun images, a typical vessel of the Dawenkou Culture, excavated at the Dawenkou Culture site

The hole on this jade shovel excavated at the Dawenkou Culture site was pierced by a fairly advanced drill. The shovel was not a tool, but a ritual object and a symbol of the power of the nobles. (from *Xintai Culture*)

The pottery *gui* (cooking tripod) found at the Dawenkou Culture site was a common cooking utensil of the Dawenkou people. It was also a representative utensil of their culture.

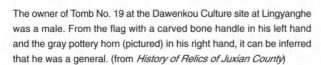

The owner of Tomb No. 19 at the Dawenkou Culture site at Lingyanghe was a male. From the flag with a carved bone handle in his left hand and the gray pottery horn (pictured) in his right hand, it can be inferred that he was a general. (from *History of Relics of Juxian County*)

Daily life of the Dawenkou people

Burning Firewood to Worship Heaven — the Oldest Rite

During the Spring and Autumn Period (770-476 BC), when Duke Huan (sovereign of the State of Qi, 685-643 BC) became a powerful ruler, united the warring dukedoms and brought peace to the country, he wanted to hold a grand ceremony on Mount Taishan to offer sacrifices to heaven. But his able official Guan Zhong told him that he had heard that 72 monarchs had previously done so but that these had all been virtuous rulers, implying that Duke Huan was not qualified to follow in their footsteps.

There's no way of proving the truth or otherwise of Guan Zhong's words, but certainly they were not entirely without foundation. The ceremony of offering sacrifices to heaven and earth on Mount Taishan was a special religious event with a long history.

China's most ancient text, the *Book of History*, describes a set of religious rites performed when Shun succeeded Yao as leader of the allied tribes in the late period of the patriarchal society. The ceremonial process included; first, worship of the supreme god, then the heavenly gods of the sun, moon and stars, and the earthly gods of the mountains, rivers and seas. The mountain here referred to the large ones on earth, the chief of which was called Daizong — meaning Mount Taishan.

The spot where 72 rulers are said to have performed mountain worship ceremonies on Mount Taishan

35

The three legendary sage kings and the five virtuous emperors of antiquity worshipping Mount Taishan

was administering affairs on earth on behalf of heaven and asking for its blessing. This ceremony was called "*chai*" (burning firewood to worship heaven).

Then, Shun would look out onto every direction one after the other. At the same time, the chieftains of all the tribes would all climb to the top of the mountains in their regions and worship toward Mount Taishan. This was called "*wang*" (gazing out to the mountains and rivers).

The ceremonial in its entirety was called "*chai wang*" and the plaque bearing the words "*chai wang yi feng*" (*chai wang* tradition) that hangs in the Jade Emperor Temple on the summit of Mount Taishan is a reminder of this most holy religious and political ceremony.

As leader of the allied tribes, Shun made an inspection tour across the whole country every five years. In spring, he inspected Daizong, or the East Sacred Mountain. In summer, he inspected the South Sacred Mountain. In autumn, the West Sacred Mountain and in winter, the North Sacred Mountain. The East Sacred Mountain was Mount Taishan, the other three are hard to identify, but they should be quite near the Yellow River.

When Shun visited Mount Taishan, he climbed to the summit and lit the ceremonial fire with his own hands. The dense smoke rose high in the sky, mingling with the clouds. Shun was sending the message to heaven, via this rising smoke, that he

Obviously, the combination of inspection tours and "*chai wang*" ceremonies was a way of controlling the allied tribes. The systemization of the practice illustrates the embryonic formation of a primitive state. By summoning different tribes and clans under the same belief in one god, and under the rule of the god's son, the ceremonial played an immense role in the formation of a commonwealth. It may be inferred that Mount Taishan inspection tours and ceremonies helped the countless tribes living by the lower Yellow River and to the north along the Pacific coast to form a vague sense of nationhood, and to develop a common, centripetal and cohesive

Burning wood to worship heaven

Bronze statue of the Jade Emperor enshrined in his temple on top of Mount Taishan

force, thus doing the temporal and spiritual groundwork, laying down cultural and philosophical foundations for these areas to grow into a nation state and to blend together as the Chinese people.

Why did these ancient rulers make Mount Taishan the foremost of mountains and the site for such grand ceremonies? The answer lies in the fact that Mount Taishan was the highest mountain in east China, allowing them to take the worship of the sun, the worship of the east, and the mountain worship of primitive religion and roll them all up into one — Mount Taishan worship. With the dawning of a civilization on the land west of the Pacific, Mount Taishan naturally became a sacred spot to the Chinese ancestors, an altar that was as close to heaven as you could get, an open palace giving the first view of the rising sun.

Legends say the Yellow Emperor visited Mount Taishan several times and worshipped earth at Tingtingshan, a hilltop northeast of today's Wenkou Town

Theoretical Roots of the "Mountain Worship" Ceremony

According to Guan Zhong, the last of the 72 ancient rulers to pay sacrifice on Mount Taishan was King Cheng, the second ruler of the Western Zhou Dynasty (11th century-771 BC) in the 11th century BC. If he was right, by the time the First Emperor of Qin (r. 221-210 BC) visited Mount Taishan in 219 BC, more than 800 years had gone by without any ceremony being held. During those eight centuries, tremendous historical changes had taken place, including a second massive integration of peoples, and the transition from slavery and dukedoms to a centralized feudal system.

In the Warring States Period, farsighted statesmen and thinkers foresaw that a new united country, superior to what had gone before, was dawning on the eastern horizon. Zou Yan, a thinker at the Jixia School in the Qi capital of Linzi, not far from Mount Taishan, put forth a theory on "*yin* and *yang* and the cycle of five virtues" that formed the theoretical foundation for the emergence of a new united country. Zou held that the country would never be ruled by one single family, and that change of rule was a result of the interaction of the five elements that controlled the universe — metal, wood, water, fire and earth. When

Cliff face inscription east of the South Gate to Heaven: "The place where all things that tower heavenwards originate."

one old dynasty declined, a vigorous new one, one more suited to needs of the times, would rise to replace it. This was acting in compliance with heaven's will.

The best way to announce to the world that rule had been transferred was to hold a ceremony on Mount Taishan. Why did it have to be Mount Taishan? One reason was that since time immemorial Mount Taishan had been the holy altar where rulers reported to heaven. The other was that since this foremost of mountains stood in the east where, according to the five-element theory, *yin* and *yang*

The open space in front of the Jade Emperor Temple on top of Mount Taishan
was where sacrificial altars were built in ancient times.

At the Heaven and Earth Square completed in recent years are 12 pillars with coiling
dragons, representing the 12 emperors who held worship ceremonies on Mount Taishan.
The square is at Tianwai Village where the road leads up to Mount Taishan.

alternated, where all things had their genesis and growth, the birth of a new dynasty should be legitimized by holding a "mountain worship" ceremony on Mount Taishan, so that the new rule would have the blessing of the heaven.

An inscription on the cliffs near the South Gate to Heaven extols Mount Taishan as the "place where all things that tower heavenwards originate." This is a good illustration of Mount Taishan's being the supreme sacred altar for the performance of sacrificial rites to heaven by ancient emperors. No other mountain in China was deemed worthy of such an honor.

The "mountain worship" ceremony of offering sacrifices to heaven and earth had the same religious and political significance as the Mount Taishan *chai wang*" ceremony, but in a changed form.

The Chinese words for "mountain worship" are "*feng shan*". Here the "*feng* element of the rite involved building soil into an altar mound on the summit, onto which the ruler would climb and pray to heaven, a sign to announce the legitimacy of his reign. Essentially it was the same as "reporting" in the "*chai wang*" ceremony.

The "*shan*" element involved a patch of land being cleared on a hill below Mount Taishan and used to express gratitude to earth. This ceremony also proclaimed the ruler's legitimate ownership of the land, mountains and rivers, and had the same connotations as the ceremony of "gazing out on the mountains and rivers."

So, we can conclude that the "*feng shan*" and "*chai wang*" ceremonies both used the name of heaven so as to declare the emperors' legitimate rule over the land and the people. Rites associating political legitimacy with the supernatural were summarized by ancient thinkers as "teaching and ruling the people by imitating the way of the gods."

The First Emperor of Qin

First Emperor of Qin Pays Homage to Mount Taishan

The first Chinese to formally conduct the "mountain worship" ceremony in accordance with the "cycle of five virtues" theory was the First Emperor of Qin, the first historical emperor of China. In the third year after he had unified China, this ruler who had risen to power in the west marched eastward with his mighty troops.

He first ascended Zouyi Hill in the southeast of Zouxian County, Shandong. Since no "mountain worship" ceremony

had been held for 800 years, neither the emperor nor his entourage had any idea of what it should be like. So the emperor called 70 Confucian scholars from the former State of Lu to discuss the rite. Confucian scholars all said that there was nothing special beyond the simple cleaning beforehand, the important thing being to show the mountain respect and reverence, without a hint of self-pride. When the rulers of antiquity had worshipped Mount Taishan, they had their carriage wheels wrapped with cattail so as to avoid harming any of its grasses, trees, rock or soil. The emperor was surprised to hear this and was reluctant to implement it. He even suspected the scholars were toying with him and so decided off his own bat to first worship on Mount Taishan and then descend from the north side to worship earth at nearby Mount Liangfu.

But the emperor was taught a lesson by the God of Mount Taishan for his arrogance and discourtesy. When he got to northwest of the imperial tent, he was caught in a downpour, so he rushed to take shelter under a big tree, which he later honored with the title *"wu da fu"* (ninth rank official during the Qin Dynasty).

In 211 BC, a year before the emperor's death, a huge meteorite fell on Mount Taishan, on which someone se-

The pine honored by the First Emperor of Qin 2,000 years ago no longer exists.

cretly carved the words: "The First Emperor of Qin dies when the land is divided." The shaken emperor immediately sent officials to investigate the case but nothing definite emerged so he ordered the killing of everyone living near the meteorite and the destruction of the meteorite itself. The following year, he died at Shaqiu (in today's Hebei Province) on his way back from an inspection tour of the east.

The First Emperor of Qin, who dreamed of the east, who had spent most of the 12 years of his reign inspecting the east, had the terracotta troops and horses in his mausoleum lined up in ranks all facing the east. Perhaps the true motive power for his unifying the whole country was in fact the magnetic pull in the east.

The First Emperor of Qin's "mountain worship" ceremony on Mount Taishan was a formal, solemn announcement of the birth of the first united empire under a central power in Chinese history. It marked the unification into a single, powerful country of the two parts of China — one facing the Asian interior in the northwest, the other facing the sea in the east. Mount Taishan was promoted from a sacred mountain worshipped by tribes in the east to one worshipped by all the peoples of China, and became a holy symbol of national unification.

Emperor Wu of the Han Dynasty

Emperor Wu's Eight Visits to Mount Taishan

In 110 BC, before setting out to pay homage on Mount Taishan, Emperor Wu (r.140-87 BC) of the Western Han Dynasty announced three pre-conditions for holding mountain worship ceremonies on the mountain: first, the whole country must be united with rebellions put down; second, there must be peace and tranquility and a long period of order and stability; and third, there must be repeated auspicious signs. Only if all three conditions were met, could a ruler be qualified to perform the ceremony.

As legend said that the Yellow Em-peror became an immortal whilst con-ducting wars on the one hand and reli-gious austerity on the other, Emperor Wu decided to set out from his capital Chang'an (present day Xi'an), with 180,000 troops, detouring via Yunyang, Shangjun, Xihe and Wuyuan in the north, then marching north beyond the Great Wall as far as Suofang and the Beihe River. While conducting this show of strength directed at the hostile nomadic Xiongnu tribe in the north, large ceremonies were also held to wor-ship the mountains on the journey east.

When he passed by the Mausoleum of the Yellow Emperor at Qiaoshan in today's Shaanxi Province, Emperor Wu heard that there was a tomb containing the personal effects of the deceased ancestor. He ordered his soldiers to carry soil to build a high terrace overnight, so that he could worship the Yellow Em-peror and pray to the immortals. On the way, he also held ceremonies on Mount Huashan and Mount Songshan, and in-spected regions by the coast, before the procession finally reached the eastern foot of Mount Taishan. After a grand cer-emony of worship at the foot of the mountain, Emperor Wu left his troops behind and ascended the mountain in a mood of mystic reverence, accompanied only by the son of the deceased General Huo Qubing. Alone on the mountain, the

The Wordless Stele on top of Mount Taishan

Cloud-patterned tile-ends excavated at the site of Immortals Watching Terrace, built on the summit after Emperor Wu worshipped the mountain

achievements, leave nothing but a blank stele on Mount Taishan? Was it that the emperor suddenly felt inferior and became modest and prudent when faced with the supreme mountain? Well, yes and no.

In ancient China, wordless steles could not be erected by simply anyone; this honor was reserved for those whose merits and virtues were boundless. Such lofty spheres were beyond expression in words, indeed words might even cause them harm. Therefore, Emperor Wu's wordless stele expressed his boundless respect and admiration to heaven, earth and Mount Taishan, and also showed his confidence and pride in his great cause. This is what is meant by "equally great as any wordy praise." The poem *Wordless Stele* by the Ming Dynasty poet Zou Depu clearly read the emperor's mind, "The stele stands blank on the steep cliff, a matchless idea of the ancients. When there is no praise, it is the best praise of all."

emperor who used to consider everything beneath his notice could not help uttering heartfelt praises of the great mountain.

The Wordless Stele on the summit has remained a historical mystery, with diverse explanations proffered, none of them convincing. After careful study of the *Records of the Historian* by Sima Qian, the official historian in the reign of Emperor Wu, Gu Yanwu, a famous 17th century scholar, concluded that the stele was erected by Emperor Wu.

Since the main purpose of the mountain worship ceremony was to report the ruler's achievements to heaven and earth, to erect a stele carved with the details should be a main part of the ceremony. Why did Emperor Wu, a brilliant ruler known for his political and military

Emperor Wu visited Mount Taishan on eight occasions. Besides the wordless stele, he also left the Mingtang Hall, a sacrificial structure on the southeast slope. The structure was built to a design proffered by an alchemist from Ji'an. In the middle of the complex is a hall covered with a thatched roof and opens on four sides, with water running through the hall on the ground. The hall is encircled by two rings of walls, with a passageway between the two, and at the southwest of the complex stands the Kunlun Tower. On every visit the emperor would climb the tower to worship in the hall and receive feudal lords here.

Building a sacrificial structure at the foot of Mount Taishan, designing the passageway and the tower like a corridor to heaven, naming it after the majestic Kunlun Mountain, holding activities to worship the heavenly god, the gods of the five directions and the ancestors ... all these things reveal Emperor Wu's true motive for visiting Mount Taishan —

Han cypresses, said to have been planted by Emperor Wu. The exuberant trees once were listed as one of the eight best sights of Tai'an.

namely to become an immortal. The emperor's concern for the world of ghosts and spirits rather than real life was laid bare when he once told his officials, "If I could ride a dragon to ascend heaven and become an immortal like the Yellow Emperor, I wouldn't hesitate one second to abandon my wives and children just like slipping off my shoes."

Apart from worshipping and receiving the feudal lords, the emperor's main aim was to meet the immortals. His obsession with visiting Mount Taishan came from the alchemists' saying that there were many immortals living there at the sacred mountain. It was said that he did encounter two of them, who even gave him a pillow stuffed with medicinal herbs. That said, the immortals failed to make the emperor live forever; he died at the age of 69, neither the longest nor the shortest lifespan of the several hundred emperors in Chinese history. Yet, the cypresses he brought from the Central Plains and planted in Temple of Mount Taishan have witnessed the tremendous changes over the past 2,000 years. Some have died and been turned into sculptures, others still flourish, even with hollow trunks and peeled-off bark.

According to the *Tai'an County Annals,* when he paid homage to Mount Taishan, Emperor Wu "had a copper-silver tripod caldron built, which was four *chi* (about 1 meter) high and in the shape of an urn. The caldron bore the inscription "When the emperor ascends Mount Taishan, all wish his majesty a long life and peace for the whole country, and this sacred caldron is built to record the event." This is the best reflection of the dual public and private objectives of the emperor's visit, but note that "a long life" went before "peace for the whole country."

For over a hundred years, the great cause of national unity pursued by both the First Emperor of Qin and Emperor Wu of Han was essentially an attempt to ensure that "all lands and waters under heaven belong to the emperor." Hence, visits by rulers to Mount Taishan virtually became a symbol of national unification. Apart from its original function of expressing gratitude to heaven and earth, the event also indicated the change from chaos to peace. As the Eastern Han Dynasty (25-220 AD) historian Ban Gu put it: "Why do rulers usually pay homage to Mount Taishan when the regime changes? To report the changes and to show the people that they have the Mandate of Heaven. At times of peace and prosperity, they also visit the mountain to report their merits."

The Ailing Emperor Guangwu Comes to Mount Taishan

After the death of Emperor Wu, there were no grand ceremonies held on Mount Taishan for more than a century. Then in the 32nd year of his reign, Liu Xiu, Emperor Guangwu of the Eastern Han Dynasty (r. 25-57), found many pretexts for his going to worship Mount Taishan, under the theme of "receiving orders to rejuvenate the country."

Interestingly enough, the lofty political and cultural significance of the grand event put great pressure on the emperor. So, when he first heard an official asking him to hold the "mountain worship" ceremony there, he was angry, "I've ruled for 30 years, and the people still have a bellyful of complaints. So who's going to be deceived? Heaven?" Ironically, it was this same Guangwu, the first Chinese emperor to recognize that the "mountain worship" ceremony should not be used to deceive the people, who was also the first, a mere two years later, to deliberately exploit the opportunity of this ancient ceremony of dialogue with the gods in order to obtain supernatural support for the legitimacy and continuation of his rule. The ailing emperor, in order that his descendents would succeed safely to the throne after his death,

planned the ceremony by himself, and set a historical precedent by inviting leaders of ethnic minorities to participate.

While the ceremonies held by the First Emperor of Qin and Emperor Wu of Han served two purposes — politics and immortality — Emperor Guangwu turned the event into a political stunt of "teaching and ruling the people by imitating the way of deities" so as to guarantee long and stable dominance by his own Liu clan. He staged the event, to awe not only people in the Central Plains and the vicinities, but also the ethnic minorities in frontier areas that mi-

Relief carving depicting Emperor Wu's ceremony of worship on Mount Taishan

ght rebel at any time. The tactic was adopted and further developed by his descendants when they held similar ceremonies on Mount Taishan. Emperor Guangwu's wish was also fulfilled after his death, since his offspring did continue his empire for more than 160 years.

After Emperor Guangwu's visit, Mount Taishan became quiet once more — in sharp contrast to the chaotic state of the country which split under different rulers. This state lasted for nearly 500 years, during which time Mount Taishan was undisturbed.

The Regrets of Tang Emperor Taizong

The wheels of history turned, reaching the seventh century, the peaceful and prosperous age of the reign of Emperor Taizong of the Tang Dynasty (618-907), when China once more stabilized after great chaos. Li Shimin, Emperor Taizong (r. 627-649), considered himself to rank among the greatest emperors in Chinese history by reason of his outstanding statesmanship, brilliant military exploits, benevolence and confidence, and thus well qualified to perform the mountain worship ceremony on Mount Taishan. However, Wei Zheng, an official known for his straight talking, poured cold water on this, reminding the emperor of the actual situation in the Central Plains and the areas around Mount Taishan, saying: "Over the vast land from east Luoyang in Henan to Mount Taishan and the East Sea, the smoke of cooking fires is hardly to be seen, the crowing of roosters and barking of dogs hardly to be heard, the roads lie in ruin, making travel very difficult.... If Your Majesty insists on holding the "*feng shan*" ceremony on Mount Taishan, all neighbors will send envoys to attend the event. But how can we invite them to those places and show them weakness and dilapidation?"

The emperor took Wei's point, but his enthusiasm for the project was not

In the early 1920s, the Chinese scholar tree planted in the Tang Dynasty in the southwest of the Temple of Mount Taishan finally died, but its replacement is thriving.

dampened; he returned to the topic on three later occasions. Finally, in 641, he issued an imperial decree, announcing that he would do something at Mount Taishan. But when his imperial carriage reached the palace at Luoyang, a comet was seen falling across the sky; this forced the large contingents to turn back, because according to ancient astronomy, comets were harbingers of war. In fact, the sudden fighting that broke out on the northwest frontier was the real reason for the cancellation en route of the planned sacrificial activity. To ancient Chinese monarchs, "Military and sacrificial matters are the two major issues of the state." Sacrifices were important, but they could take time to plan, whilst war was more important and urgent in terms of the safety of the nation. The cancellation of the planned ceremony severely disappointed Emperor Taizong.

However, his thwarted ambition was finally fulfilled by his son Li Zhi and Wu Zetian, originally Taizong's concubine but later to become his daughter-in-law.

Emperor and Empress Together Make Sacrifices to Mount Taishan

In the tenth month of 665, Li Zhi, Emperor Gaozong (r. 650-683), leading a retinue of officials and generals, and his empress Wu Zetian at the head of a large contingent of concubines and noble ladies, set out east toward Mount Taishan. The emperor himself was physically weak and politically indecisive, so the grand mountain worship event was actually planned by his ambitious wife Wu Zetian.

Among the long procession were envoys from the three kingdoms on the Korean Peninsula, from Japan, India, Persia, and other neighboring regimes in Xinjiang, as well as chiefs of southwestern tribes, together with their large tented carriages, cattle and camels. Inviting so many guests to the ceremony obviously had a political agenda, namely strengthening the Tang court's relationship with ethnic minorities and neighboring countries and demonstrating China's prosperity, stability and unity. This was very different from Emperor Wu of Han leading an 180,000-strong force to Mount Taishan, in order to intimidate, along his way, the northern nomadic tribe of Xiongnu.

The several-hundred-kilometer-long procession — the world's mightiest, most luxurious and magnificent — traveled for two months before gathering at the foot of Mount Taishan, when it was already the first month of the following year. On an auspicious day, the emperor first worshipped heaven on Mount Taishan, then went to offer sacrifices to earth at Sheshou Mountain. Following the emperor, the empress ascended the sacrificial altar to pay her homage, and then it was the turn of another concubine to wrap up the sacrificial ceremony — an unprecedented and unimagined scene. Ignoring the disguised laughter of sniggering officials, Wu Zetian and the concubine went through the formalities in all solemnity. Wu's struggle resulted in women participating and officiating at the grand "*feng shan*" ceremony for the very first time in Chinese history; and for the first time ever too, a state ceremony actualized the Chinese philosophical theories of the productive union of male and female forces — heaven and earth, *yin* and *yang*, force and grace....

At the Temple of Mount Taishan, people can find a most unusual stele; it consists of two identical tablets, lined up against each other and sharing a single stone capital and a single base. This "Double Stone Stele" was erected in 661 when Emperor Gaozong and Empress Wu Zetian sent Taoist priests to build statues on Mount Taishan. The rare form symbolized Wu Zetian and Li Zhi's joint reign and their deep mutual love, like loyal mandarin ducks; because of this it is nicknamed the "Mandarin Duck Stele." The stele can also be seen as further testimony to Chinese women's successful struggle for equal political power.

Aside from the first ever participation of women in state ceremonial, 31 years later Wu Zetian worked another miracle; for the first and only time in Chinese history, she, as the only female monarch in China, presided over a sacrificial ceremony on Mount Songshan in Henan Province, the Central of the Five Sacred Mountains, a rite which posed the first ever challenge to Mount Taishan's centuries-old status as supreme among the five sacred mountains.

According to historical records, different emperors followed different rituals

The Double Stone Stele erected in 661

when staging the "*feng shan*" ceremony. The procedures followed by Emperor Gaozong in the first month of 666 first involved the building of altars.

The first altar, called Fengsi Alter, was built two kilometers south of Mount Taishan. It consisted of three circular mounds, the east, south, west, north sides and center of which were covered with soils of representative colors — blue, red, white, black and yellow respectively.

The next alter, called Dengfeng Altar, was built on the summit of Mount Taishan, three meters high and 56 square meters in area.

The third alter, called Jiangshan Altar, was built on Sheshou Mountain.

In addition, there was the Chaojin Altar, or Pilgrimage Alter, built at the foot of Mount Taishan.

So, Emperor Gaozong in the year of 666 had four altars built for the ceremony.

The ceremony started at the first alter, Fengsi Altar, where the emperor worshipped and offered sacrifices to the god of heaven, when the memorial tablets of his grandfather and father were also placed on the sides to receive obeisance. A jade document, inscribed with the emperor's prayer to the god, was stamped with the imperial seal and ink paste before being placed in a stone casket and packed and sealed up with five-colored soil.

The following day, the emperor ascended the mountain to worship the god of heaven at Dengfeng Altar, accompanied by the memorial tablet of his grandfather. This was the main part and climax of the whole ceremony. The emperor ascended the altar from the south and stood facing the north. Then, a senior imperial minister knelt down and took the jade document out of the stone case and placed it on the sacrificial table. After making obeisance, the emperor also knelt down and put the jade document into a jade chest, then tied the chest with a gold thread, applied the imperial ink paste, and stamped the paste with a special seal inscribed with two characters: "*shou ming*," meaning with heavenly mandate. Then the emperor, still kneeling, passed the jade chest on to the minister, who then placed it on the table for the emperor to make obeisance once more. Then the minister, on his knees, offered up the jade chest, and put it into a stone case, and an attendant put on a stone cover. Next, the emperor again tied the case with a gold thread, sealed it up it, stamped it with the "*shou ming*" seal and conducted it down the altar. Finally the attendant sealed the stone case with five-colored mud, and it was placed on a firewood stack, which was set alight to send a message to heaven. As the smoke curled skywards, all believed that the secret prayer inscribed on the jade document was being delivered to heaven. The cheers of everyone, those on the mountain and those below, resounded

After the mountain worship ceremony, Tang Emperor Gaozong had three steles built on Mount Taishan — Dengfeng, Jiangshan and Chaojin. The Dengfeng stele (pictured) stands on Grand View Peak at the summit; a similar one stands east of the Red Gate Palace at the foot of the mountain.

through the deep valleys.

After this ceremony, the emperor, accompanied by his officials, went to worship the god of earth at the Jiangshan Altar on Mount Sheshou. The memorial tablets of his grandfather's and father's empresses also received homage from their royal heir, as well as from Wu Zetian and the imperial concubine.

Then, after a day's rest, the emperor and his empress received officials at the Chaojin Altar and ordered that the event be commemorated by the building of three steles — Dengfeng, Jiangshan and Chaojin — and the re-naming of three altars (Dengfeng, Jiangshan and Chaojin) as respectively, "Crane Dancing Terrace," "Long Life Terrace" and "Viewing the Clouds Terrace." The emperor also announced that his reign title would be changed to "Qianfeng."

Emperor Xuanzong Comes to Mount Taishan

The decision of Li Longji, Emperor Xuanzong (r. 712-756), to perform *"feng shan"* sacrifice on Mount Taishan in the year 725 was not unrelated to Wu Zetian. Empresss Wu had taken control of the great Tang Dynasty created by the Li clan, changed its title to Zhou and declared herself emperor in her own right. Now Emperor Xuanzong, believing it was incumbent upon him to notify heaven that he had

Jade document recording Tang Emperor Xuanzong's worship of Mount Taishan

fulfilled his mission of rejuvenating the Tang Dynasty, and that the prosperous age he had brought about during his Kaiyuan reign period (713-741) was great enough to let his ancestors rest in peace, thought he must offer sacrifices on Mount Taishan to express gratitude to heaven "for the benefit of his offspring and the common people alike."

Before setting out, the emperor asked He Zhizhang, a renowned scholar of rites,

why all previous emperors were so secretive about their jade documents instead of making them public. The scholar replied: "The jade document contained what the emperor wanted only god to know — his prayer to live and reign for eternity. This is the explanation for all the secrecy." "But I only want to pray for the common people, and have no secret prayer for myself," said the emperor, who immediately ordered his jade document announced to the public. With this decision Emperor Xuanzong did away with the mysterious, immortality-seeking aura that pervaded the mountain worship ceremony.

The emperor also had his *Inscriptions in Memory of Mount Taishan* engraved on the cliff by the Grand View Peak; the 1,000-word inscription covers an area 13.3 meters high and 5.7 meters wide. The huge scale of this golden inscription has won fame as "one of earth's great sights." Embellished by Tang scholars, the text is elegant and majestic to read. Instead of selfishly praying for himself like previous rulers, Emperor Xuanzong tried to "move the god by my sincerity to grant blessings to my people." He warns: "Benevolent rule depends on political integrity, pursuing selfish desires does not bring reputation."

Ironically, considering the emperor's conduct in his later years, people may heave a sigh at his lengthy declaration of wisdom, and ponder the question why al-

Of all the steles recording imperial mountain worship ceremonies on Mount Taishan, the one bearing *Inscription in Memory of Mount Taishan* on Grand View Peak is the best preserved.

"Father-in-Law Peak" inscription on the summit

most all Chinese emperors who performed great deeds when young, became muddle-headed in old age, their actions completely contradicting their earlier ideals, many even ruining the cause that they themselves created, their legacy a shame to history.

It was not only imperial rulers who sought private gain in the name of the sacred ceremony; accompanying officials also exploited the event for personal benefit. It was alleged that Zhang Yue, who was in charge of the ceremony, abused his power by promoting his son-in-law Zheng Yi from a ninth rank to fifth rank official, the minimum rank allowed under Tang regulations to attend the ceremony. Hearing this, Emperor Xuanzong, who at this time was not yet senile, quizzed Zhang what made Zheng rise so rapidly. Zhang faltered, and a quick-witted official explained for him; "Through the power of Mount Taishan." Though the emperor did not dig any deeper, everyone was clear that it was attributable to father-in-law power, not Mount Taishan power!

Thus, "Mount Taishan" became another term for "father-in-law." Later, some-one referring to this, wrote the satirical inscription "Father-in-law Peak" on a huge rock on top of Mount Taishan.

Emperor Xuanzong's mountain worship ceremony was extremely luxurious and extravagant. The train of horses alone numbered tens of thousands, with horses of the same color forming one square phalanx, and all of them together forming a huge colorful piece of tapestry. Such extravagance was no doubt hugely wasteful and onerous for the people, but it demonstrated the power of the state to foreign countries, achieving diplomatic results that could not be won by war. The Tujue was the most powerful of the ethnic minority regimes and the Tujue rulers had a grudge against the Tang court. Aware of this, Emperor Xuanzong specially invited Tujue envoys to the ceremony. Hearing that even Tujue had sent envoys, other minority rulers also dispatched their people to the event.

To convince the minority envoys of the Tang emperor's being the son of heaven and to reinforce the mystery of the sacrificial event, the emperor and his advisors played a trick on them. On their return journey to Chang'an, the official responsible for observing astronomical phenomenon suddenly announced that a solar eclipse would take place in a few days. In ancient China, a solar eclipse was deemed an omen of disaster, possibly fatal to the emperor. Shocked by the forecast, the escorting officials and generals and the troops began striking, with all their might, anything capable of producing sound in an attempt to drive away the heavenly dog that legend said might swallow the sun. The emperor performed ritual ablution, abstained from eating and sleeping, and seriously reflected on his own misconduct. Thanks, seemingly, to all these efforts, when the time came, the sun shone brightly in the clear sky, and there was no solar eclipse at all. Everyone was reassured and the soldiers shouted "Long Live the Emperor." The minority envoys were so bamboozled by this play-acting that they were convinced the Tang emperor enjoyed the special favor of the god and therefore, "not one dared not to submit."

In some sense, the *"feng shan"* ceremony on Mount Taishan was a type of diplomatic psychological war game.

After the ceremony, Emperor Xuanzong ennobled the God of Mount Taishan with the title "Tian Qi Wang" (King Equal of Heaven). This was the first formal title to Mount Taishan recorded in official history. After this, at the same time Mount Taishan began to be made divine it also started to be personalized. Thus, this mountain that, in the primitive religion of ancient Chinese, had been associated with the mighty power of heaven and earth, was given the image of an earthly ruler, its function becoming more and more secular. This mountain, which the First Emperor of Qin and Emperor Wu of Han had held in such awe, was now granted a title by an emperor. The sacred status of Mount Taishan, a status based on the worship of the god of heaven and the Sun God, worship of the east and worship of the mountain, began to be shaken and downgraded in the face of the supreme human monarch.

For the next 200 years or so, no emperor showed interest in holding a similar ceremony on Mount Taishan. As people became more rational and as the centralized feudal system further developed, the event's primitive religious connotations and the superstitious pursuit of immortality no longer appealed to rulers; few still believed the theories of "the cycle of five virtues" and "the grace of the god"; all the extravagance with thousands of horses and carriages heading for the mountain, the emperor's exaggeration of his deeds and prayers for immortality were sneered at by people of insight as foolish and ridiculous acts. Rationally speaking, the curtain should have come down *"feng shan"* ceremony, but then, many lofty and solemn events in history eventually end up as slapstick comedy.

The end of the mountain worship ceremony on Mount Taishan had to wait until the farce performed by Zhao Heng, known as Emperor Zhenzong, of the Song Dynasty (r. 998-1022).

The Final Performance of "*Feng Shan*"

In 1004, a battle was fought at Chanzhou (southwest Puyang, Henan) between the Song court and the Liao Dynasty (907-1125), a regime established by the Qidan people in the north. The Song army won a decisive battle and the Liao troops sued for peace. The cowardly Song emperor, over-anxious to reach a peace agreement and secure an immediate enemy withdrawal, ordered his victorious army to sign the Chanyuan Treaty, which prescribed that the Song court should pay annual tributes of silver and silk to the Liao court! This set a ridiculous example of the victor paying annual compensation to the loser. To calm the ire of both officials and people, and to divert political attention generally, also to intimidate the Liao rulers and to consolidate the diplomatic results of the treaty, Emperor Zhenzong agreed to the suggestion from his pro-peace official Wang Qinruo and staged a grand "*feng shan*" ceremony on Mount Taishan as a way of conning the officials and appeasing the people.

The ceremony held by Emperor Zhenzong was the final performance of "*feng shan*" in history. Although it was pure farce, the cast gave a great performance; the plot was absurd, the direction excellent, the acting convincing, and the audience enthusiastic. There was nothing like it before or since.

Its chief director was Wang Qinruo, a true master-hand at putting on a serious performance of what had started as a joke. His directorial principles were: big budget, epic scale and the participation of a super-star. He believed that so long as a lie was "told as big as heaven," everyone would believe it, no matter how absurd.

First, he took advantage of the emperor's fear of war and made him will-

Song Emperor Zhenzong proclaimed the day that the "heavenly instructions" fell (the 6th day of the 6th lunar month) as "Heavenly Gift Festival" and had a temple (pictured) built on the spot to store the instructions. (from *Hundred Years of Mount Taishan*)

ing to play the only leading role.

With the cooperation of the super-star, the emperor, Wang designed a daring plot, seemingly unworried about how inferior it was. His key stage props were three pieces of yellow silk, the so-called "heavenly instructions." He had two of them "fall" right onto the roof of the imperial palace, the third one onto Mount Taishan. As expected, such an auspicious sign that bluntly revealed the intentions of heaven stirred court and commoner alike. Next, Wang began to mobilize and organize mass performers to take the stage in succession. Apart from officials and generals, most of the performers were ordinary people representing "the will of the people." First he had 1,200 old people from Mount Taishan and Yanzhou, the location of the Confucius Mansion, to petition before the imperial palace, asking the emperor to offer sacrifices to heaven and earth on Mount Taishan. Next up were 840 senior intellectuals (successful candidates in the highest imperial examinations), and they were followed by an even larger contingent of 24,370 people, including prestigious scholars, army generals, religious personages, representatives of ethnic minorities and people of great old age, who all went to the open space before the imperial palace, demanding that the emperor pay homage to Mount Taishan.

Stele erected at the Temple of Mount Taishan in 1013, recording Song Emperor Zhenzong's granting to the God of Mount Taishan the title of "Emperor Equal of Heaven"

After more than six months of build-up, the main character finally entered the stage. Emperor Zhenzong made a formal announcement that he would visit Mount Taishan in the following 10th month of the year.

Thanks to the pre-publicity the play was widely known before it started; the whole country was stirred up with sacrificial fever. Hordes of people, from Mount Hengshan in the north to the Yangtze and Huaihe rivers in the south, ignoring the long journey, came along, bringing their young and their old, in the hope of attending the spectacular event

Song Dynasty inscriptions of "Head of the Five Sacred Mountains" on top of Mount Taishan

at Mount Taishan. After all the last *"feng shan"* ceremony by Tang Emperor Xuanzong had been 283 years previously; the entire nation was anticipating the magnificent sight, hoping the national jubilation would inspire their jaded nerves and wash away the shadow cast by years of war.

When golden autumn fell, Emperor Zhenzong set out from Bianjing (today's Kaifeng, Henan Province) toward Mount Taishan.

Unlike all previous ceremonies, Zhenzong did not have the altar built at the top of the mountain, but at the Sun Viewing Peak; the time of worship was also different, at dawn. In order to get to the peak before sunrise, the emperor began to climb the mountain the night before. He got to the Yunbu (Cloud Step) Bridge at midnight, and had the imperial tent erected by the waterfall so that he could fall asleep to the murmuring of the spring. Before dawn, he arrived at Qinguan Peak, where he changed his clothes before being carried in a sedan chair to the Sun Viewing Peak.

Legends said that clouds gathered and big wind blew up that very night, scaring the official in charge of weather forecasts out of his wits. But the clouds dispersed and the wind stopped once the emperor ascended the mountain with the "heavenly instructions."

When the red sun rose from the east as expected, Emperor Zhenzong, dressed like the God of Mount Taishan enshrined in the Tiankuang (Heavenly Blessing) Hall, wearing his ceremonial robe and carrying a tapering jade tablet, slowly ascended the Sun Viewing Peak, against the bright sunshine and the rosy clouds. He saluted the rising sun in the most solemn manner and prayed: "May my country be peaceful and wars cease. May there be favorable weather for bumper harvests. May my people live a rich life without fear." To the enthusiastic cheers of spectators from all over the country, the rare birds and animals presented by various localities were set free onto the mountain. The emperor proclaimed a general amnesty and named the top of Mount Taishan "Heavenly Peace Summit."

Clearly, this ceremony was different from those of the Han and Tang dynasties. But why did Zhenzong choose to salute to the east at dawn on the Sun Viewing Peak? That was a secret known only to the emperor and a few officials.

One of the aims of the event was to take advantage of the Qidan people's worship of the Sun God to deter the Liao court. Just think about it: If the emperor of the Song Dynasty was standing on the Sun Viewing Peak on the East Sacred Mountain, whispering with the Sun God and thus gaining special favors and bless-

ings from the god, would the Liao court not hesitate before attacking their southern neighbor?

The practice of holding one's own sacrificial ceremony in accordance with the enemy's customs has been ridiculed and criticized by historians. Chen Bangzhan, author of the *History of the Song Dynasty*, commented that for a regime to ape the superstitious behavior of the enemy instead of trying to build a strong force to defeat it was the worst possible method.

The main beneficiary of this *"feng shan"* farce, directed by Wang Qinruo, starring the emperor, and with the whole country as "extras," was actually the God of Mount Taishan — apart, that is, from officials and generals who all went up a rank and the whole nation who stayed drunk for three days. For more than 200 years the God of Mount Taishan had remained King Equal of Heaven, a title bestowed by the Tang Emperor Xuanzong, but at last the Song Emperor Zhenzong promoted it Emperor Equal of

Heaven, and it was later nicknamed Emperor of East Sacred Mountain. His palace was also upgraded from a prince's residence to an emperor's palace, built strictly in accordance with imperial style. Tiankuang Hall, the main hall, was the only mountain god palace in China built to standards identical to those of the supreme hall in the imperial residence, with a hip roof, double eaves, nine bays wide and five bays deep. It was said that the hall's 3.3-meter-high, 62-meter-long mural depicting the inspection tour of the God of Mount Taishan was based on the style and extravagance of Emperor Zhenzong's visit to the mountain.

The mural *God of Mount Taishan on an Inspection Tour* has a total of 697 figures, in addition to forests, mountains, buildings, bridges, auspicious animals and treasures, with fine composition and use of space to constitute a masterpiece of Taoist mural painting.

The Ming Emperors and Mount Taishan

Emperor Zhenzong's trip to Mount Taishan failed to stop the northern cavalry from treading on the Central Plains, but the Han Chinese ultimately overthrew the Yuan regime established by the nomadic people. In theory, Zhu Yuanzhang, Emperor Taizu of the Ming Dynasty (1368-1644) who drove out the Mongols and restored Han rule was great enough to hold the "*feng shan*" ceremony on Mount Taishan. But what awaited the mountain was an imperial edict to strip the mountain of its "emperor" title.

The stele marking the cancellation of Mount Taishan's emperor title was erected at the decree of Emperor Taizu in the third year of his reign (1368-1398). As the rulers of the Tang, Song and Yuan dynasties had conferred on the God of Mount Taishan supreme titles, making it equal to the real emperor, it threatened the supreme authority of the Ming monarch. "As there is but one sun in the sky, so there can be only one unrivalled ruler in one country." Fully aware of this, shortly after ascending the throne, Zhu Yuanzhang annulled all previous titles granted to Mount Taishan, and demoted it from Emperor of East Sacred Mountain to its original status as a mountain god.

Furthermore, Zhu thought the sacrificial ceremony absurd and expressed his clear intention not to hold similar ceremonies, making Mount Taishan no longer as sacred and mysterious as it had been. Encouraged by the emperor, Ming Dynasty scholars not only took Mount Taishan a place for sightseeing, but also dared enough to leave their own poems and inscriptions on the cliffs. On the sub-

Stele in the Temple of Mount Taishan, recording the annulment of Mount Taishan's emperor title

ject of *"feng shan"* ceremonies that had gone before, one arrogant scholar commented: "If the climax of a heroic cause amounts to no more than building sacrificial altars on Mount Taishan, why bother fighting desperately for the throne?"

Though none of the Ming emperors actually visited Mount Taishan, it does not follow that the mountain had no sacred place in their hearts. According to Ming laws and institutions, major ceremonies and events such as the enthronement of a new emperor, the wedding of the emperor, news of triumphs, major construction projects and illnesses of the princes had to be reported immediately to Mount Taishan by high-ranking officials or eunuchs. Why? Did the God of Mount Taishan have the power to solve all these problems for the monarch? Most definitely not, but it did provide a kind of mental comfort. Whether Mount Taishan was an emperor, a king or an ordinary mountain god, it was deep-seated national belief that peace at Mount Taishan would lead to peace in the country. This belief remained entrenched, irrespective of titles. As the mountain that guarded the state, Mount Taishan had always been

Iron tower in the rear courtyard of the Temple of Mount Taishan, cast in 1533. Only the bottom three of its original 13 stories now survive. It was moved here from the Heavenly Instruction Temple

a support for the rulers.

Though the final curtain had gone down on the mountain worship ceremony with Emperor Zhenzong, and no other emperor had attempted a revival performance, the mountain's historical status as head of the Five Sacred Mountains did not change at all. No new mountain worship ceremonies were held, but other worship and sacrificial activities still continued there because what the state ceremony symbolized was the lofty political achievement of national stability and unification. Even without *"feng shan,"* Mount Taishan still stood proud as the guardian mountain of the state, nor did its symbolic role of state prosperity, peace and national unity vanish. There is no other mountain in the world that has been held in reverence by rulers of all dynasties over centuries, that has been a political symbol for a whole nation and a spiritual idol for hundreds of millions of people.

The bronze pavilion in the rear courtyard of the Temple of Mount Taishan is also a Ming Dynasty structure, built in 1615 and originally located in the Bixia Temple on the summit.

Emperor Kangxi and Mount Taishan

The love and respect for Mount Taishan shown by Emperor Kangxi and Emperor Qianlong of the Qing Dynasty (1644-1911), the last dynasty in Chinese history, was no less than that of the First Emperor of Qin and Emperor Wu of Han, but these two Qing rulers, who brought

Emperor Kangxi of the Qing Dinasty

about a flourishing age, showed more reason and understanding, less zealotry in their behavior.

Emperor Kangxi (r. 1662-1722) made his first trip to Mount Taishan in the winter of 1684. The Qing court was established by the Manchu people who lived in what is now northeast China. In the early days after taking control of the Central Plains, they encountered frequent rebellions by the Han people and the Qing rulers were kept busy suppressing insurgencies and loyalists of the previous dynasty. By the time of Emperor Kangxi, the country was reunited, the three frontier tribe rebellions had been put down, and the Penghu Islands and the island of Taiwan had reverted to the motherland from foreign occupation. Thus, the emperor decided to tour the south as a way to consolidate his rule of the Han people and win over the support of the Han gentry in terms of politics and culture.

His first destination was Mount Taishan. Having read Chinese classics and historical books, Kangxi was fully aware of the great mountain's status in the heart of the Han people. He knew that to make the Han people recognize that the Qing court had been established "by the grace of the god," he must bend his noble head before the great mountain. So he first knelt down and kowtowed to the God of Mount Taishan enshrined in the

Tiankuang Hall, then took the pains to climb to the top where he followed the ancient rite of *"chai wang,"* burning firewood to worship heaven.

Kangxi made a second visit to Mount Taishan in spring of 1703. It was his sixth tour to the south and also the last in his life. This time, he inspected the dykes of the Yellow River. An erudite 18th century scholar,

On his three visits to the mountain, Emperor Kangxi stayed in the East Imperial Hall in Temple of Mount Taishan.

Kangxi was known for his scientific studies. Before this second trip, he had made a careful study of the mountain, and was quite disappointed. According to geomancers, Mount Huashan was the tiger and Mount Taishan was the dragon, and the geographers also held that the screen-like peaks of Mount Taishan were its wings, but no one had ever indicated where the dragon's head was. Utilizing the geographical knowledge and measurement skills he had learned from foreign missionaries, Kangxi made an attentive study of the terrain and even ordered navigation surveys conducted. Finally he came to the conclusion that Mount Taishan had originated from the Changbai Mountain in northeast China.

Kangxi's essay "The Origin of Mount Taishan" was not written for purely scientific motives, nor to explore China's geomorphology, but in order to find a geomantic basis for Manchu rule over the Central Plains supported by the origination of the sacred Mount Taishan. Since the Changbai Mountain and the Heilongjiang River were said to be the auspicious original place of the Manchu people, the association of Mount Taishan with the Changbai Mountain was at least a powerful argument for Manchu rule to the Han people who sincerely believed in geomantic omens. The remarkable thing is that, from what we now know about geological structure, Kangxi's conclusion was not just fantasy; there is in fact a relationship between Mount Taishan and the Changbai Mountain and the north, north-east stretching New Cathaysian structural system.

Qianlong, the Last Monarch to Visit Mount Taishan

In 1748, Emperor Qianlong (r.1736-1795) made his first visit to Mount Taishan. Strongly impressed by the mountain, the talented emperor sighed with emotion, "What a great mountain it is. For centuries, it has been standing guard over this vast land. So admiring, does the mountain have a poem written on its cliff?"

While ascending the mountain, the emperor enjoyed the changing scenery and conceived his odes to the sacred image. He suddenly realized that learning and self-attainment were both like sightseeing while climbing; one should not stick to a single point and be content with what has already been attained. Immersed in his thinking, he arrived at Chaoyang Cave. Looking around, he saw the surrounding ridges rising and falling, the main peak standing to the north, a stream winding down the mountain east of the Eighteen Bends, the Pine of Welcome spreading its branches over the grotesque rocks and the white clouds. The emperor acclaimed, with a tinge of regret: What a marvelous scroll painting! How could

Poetry by the Qing Emperor Qianlong on the Yufeng Cliff

there be no painter's seal stamped on such a beautiful picture? So, he composed his thoughts into a poem and had it inscribed on the cliff east of the cave.

Known as "Huge Stele," the inscription of the emperor's poem is 20 meters high and 9 meters wide, with each character 1 meter long. The characters are cut in intaglio and colored in with red and the entire work looks like a huge seal on the natural scroll painting of Mount Taishan.

Of all the ancient monarchs, Qianlong's attitude toward the mountain was the most "modern." On one

Emperor Qianlong visited Mount Taishan ten times and left 130-odd steles and poems. Pictured here is a stele beside the Han cypresses in the Temple of Mount Taishan.

hand, he continued the long historical tradition of mountain worship, while on the other he made it clear that he had no intention of holding the *"feng shan"* ceremony himself. Regarding his personal relation with Mount Taishan, his roles changed on different trips: as head of the state he prayed that the people should have good harvests; as a dutiful son he prayed for longevity for his mother; as a scholar he pondered on the origin of mountain-worship customs and their significance for state politics. But for the most part he came as a poet who loved the fabulous landscape. This productive emperor made 10 trips to the mountain, climbing to the top on six occasions and leaving 140 poems and 130 stele

71

inscriptions. Though few of them are excellent works, they clearly reveal his strong interest in the mountain.

In the third month of 1790, as spring flowers were blooming, Emperor Qianlong made an inspection tour to Mount Taishan in celebration of his 80th birthday. He visited the Temple of Mount Taishan, climbed to the summit and offered sacrifices to the god of Yuanjun. After that, he feasted the accompanying officials and rewarded the troops. He even ordered that all the prefectures and counties he passed between Tai'an (where Mount Taishan is located) and the capital Beijing should be exempted from tax and that silver be granted to people living in the Mount Taishan region. This was his sixth and last visit to the top of Mount Taishan. As his doddering figure faded in the distance, an invisible door of history closed behind him, and Mount Taishan said farewell to the last emperor to kneel before it.

One hundred and twenty years later, the heavy door of history was closed in the Forbidden City, as China's last dynasty was declared finished. The centuries-old relationship between

Mount Taishan and many emperors came to a final end.

Since then, Mount Taishan has become the people's mountain and will continue to be worshipped by millions of Chinese forever.

Among the rare offerings the emperors presented to Mount Taishan were two lions carved from fragrant agalloch eaglewood, and a pointed jade tablet (both produced during the reign of the Qing of Emperor Qianlong) and a yellow and blue porcelain calabash vase (made by the Ming imperial kiln). Together they are known as "The Three Treasures of Mount Taishan."

Chapter III

The Universe in Miniature

The Central Mountain — A Pillar Leading to Heaven

Our ancestors crossed the Pamirs Highland long, long ago, and our vision today goes far beyond the geographical area of "the Central Plains." Today we know that the roof of the world is in Tibet and man has conquered the Qomolangma (Mount Everest), the world's highest mountain, time and time again. Man has even walked upon the Moon. However, at the early stages of Chinese civilization, our predecessors inhabiting the vast Central Plains knew only that "Of the beautiful mountains in Central China, none can compare with Mount Taishan." For a long time, Mount Taishan was considered the highest and biggest mountain at the center of the earth. And to the primitive thinking of our ancestors, it was a pillar leading to heaven.

People of very remote antiquity had the concept that the earth was one single landmass surrounded by seas, called Qizhou. It was just like the navel of the earth, and with the navel being at the center of the human body, thus Qizhou was also the center of the earth. Hence their belief, "Qizhou surrounded by seas is called the Central Kingdom."

About 100 million years ago, alluvial mud and sand brought by the Yellow, Haihe and Huaihe rivers formed a plain embraced by mountains in the north, south and west. Ancient people called these connected mountain screens *yue* (meaning high mountains), hence the concepts of North Mountain, South Mountain and West Mountain. At the center of the vast and fertile plain encircled by the three mountains stood one high mountain, regarded as the Heavenly Pillar Peak stationed right between heaven and earth. This was Mount Taishan.

Mount Taishan, standing tall and soaring into the heaven, was a sacred mountain to the people of the Central Kingdom of Qi.

Empress Wu Zetian once wanted to confer a title upon Mount Taishan. Although Mount Songshan had become the Central Sacred Mountain of the five, she still conferred the title "Tian Zhong Wang" (Central King of Heaven) on Mount Taishan. When Emperor Xuanzong of Tang performed the mountain worship ceremony on Mount Taishan, he changed its title to "Tian Qi Wang" (King Equal to Heaven). Later Emperor Zhenzong of Song promoted it to "Tian Qi Ren Sheng Di" (Virtuous and Sacred Emperor Equal to Heaven). These titles were all conferred upon Mount Taishan after the Five Sacred Mountains system had taken shape and after Mount Taishan had become the universally known Sacred Eastern Mountain. Evidently these emperors and their erudite officials were still willing to respect history. Perhaps they wanted to wrap their "*feng shan*" ceremony with a more sacred Mandate of Heaven aura, with Mount Taishan as a heavenly staircase at the navel of heaven and earth. At the top, a place enveloped in cloud and fog was Heaven Paradise, where the Emperor of Heaven lived.

Some scholars believe that Mount Taishan is possibly the Mount Kunlun in ancient Chinese mythology.

Mount Kunlun was the most mysterious mountain in ancient Chinese mythology. Its status can be compared to that of Mount Olympus in Greek mythology, also inhabited by a supreme god and lesser gods.

Mount Kunlun was a mountain leading to heaven, and it had three levels:

The first level was called Dunqiu, inhabited by immortals.

The second, called Xuanpu, was inhabited by deities able to summon wind and rain.

The third was called Tianting (Heavenly Court), inhabited by the Emperor of Heaven, ruler of everything in heaven and earth.

Mount Taishan was such a sacred mountain; its three levels of heavenly realms were reached by the First Gate to Heaven, the Mid-way Gate to Heaven and South Gate to Heaven.

The axis ascending Mount Taishan starts from the Heavenly Street south of the Double Dragon Pool.

Divine Song to Heaven

What ancient myth called the three levels of heavenly realms are actually three layers of geological faults. The three geological fault layers at Mount Taishan are a phenomenon of nature that provided man with the natural conditions to imagine paradise, but the design of the axis bestriding the three faults, from mountain foot to mountain summit, through valleys, buildings and winding paths, was a very deliberate, conscious cultural act.

The grand plan of this cultural act was to open up a road between the human world and heaven on the axis of the towering holy Mount Taishan, and through a progressive and inspiring rhythm link heaven, earth and man in order, performing a solemn and majestic divine song to heaven.

The axis chosen was Zhongxi Stream on the mountain's south flank since the three oblique geographical faults of Mount Taishan were all on its southern side, and the axis could thread from top to bottom through the bench terrain formed by the three faults.

Aerial view of the Temple of Mount Taishan

To the south of Mount Taishan was a vast expanse of cultivated land — Wenyang and Guiyin of the State of Lu. "Mount Taishan is lofty and magnificent, the State of Lu looks up at it with reverence." The land, densely populated and built up, was where pilgrims to Mount Taishan rested up, packed, assembled and dispersed.

The design of the axis had to take into consideration how to link the nearby city of Tai'an into the mountain.

The Temple of Mount Taishan became a symbol. It became the center of Tai'an City, and contrasted with the summit of Mount Taishan, forming a unique scene.

The north-south axis starts at Tongtian Street, runs through the Memorial Archway for Mount Taishan to the First Gate to Heaven, and then extends to the summit of Mount Taishan along the path running parallel with the Zhongxi Stream.

Mount Taishan's major buildings stand in order along the axis or on either sides. The spaces are ordered in a specific sequence along this vertical line. It is like a magnificently structured, exquisite and meticulous symphony on the theme of paying respects to heaven, an inspiring "divine song" of immense sweep, unfolding verse by verse.

Tongtian Street is the prelude to the "divine song." Straight road, low houses, and busy town streetscape — a flourishing secular scene.

At the end of Tongtian Street is a majestic palace — the Temple of Mount Taishan, ancestor temple of all the temples to the God of Mount Taishan in China.

The palace maintains more or less the layout of those of the Song Dynasty and was built to the scale and shape of an imperial city. Right at the center of the south side is Zhengyang Gate, Luzhan Gate on the north side, Qingyang Gate on the east and Sujing Gate on the west. The palace

The Archway of the Temple of Mount Taishan stands in front of Zhengyang (Sun Facing) Gate, the main gate of the temple. It is the largest extant stone archway on Mount Taishan. Built in 1672, it has four columns and is covered with delicate relief carvings.

city is surrounded by high city walls with a watchtower standing at each of its four corners. Within its boundary walls stand luxuriant woods and many monuments. On the axis are numerous buildings with vermilion gates, jade steps and golden halls, and a long paved path leads to the center of the palace — a three-level platform. The Tiankuang (Heavenly Blessing) Hall, the

Tiankuang Hall (Hall of Heavenly Blessing) built in the Song Dynasty enshrines the God of Mount Taishan. On its east, west and north walls of the interior is a 3.3-meter-tall and 62-meter-long mural called God of Mount Taishan Returning to the Palace.

A horizontal board bearing the words "Maintaining Stability for Heaven"

main building of the Temple of Mount Taishan, sits on the high base.

Tiankuang Hall was originally built when Emperor Zhenzong of Song went to Mount Taishan to perform the mountain worship ceremony and has been rebuilt several times since then. It follows the Nine-five principle for hip roofed buildings — i.e., a width of nine bays and a depth of five bays. The chapter Qian in

The God of the Eastern Sacred Mountain of Mount Taishan enshrined in the Hall of Heavenly Blessing

Thriving ancient trees and solemn monument stele in the Temple of Mount Taishan

the ancient book of divination, the *Book of Changes*, has such an explanation saying that "In the lines Nine and Five, a dragon flies in the field." Later generations interpret it thus: the *Yang* element is so strong that it soars to the sky, and in the same way, a sage is so virtuous that he takes the imperial throne. Therefore "Nine-five" refers to the imperial throne and a hall of these dimensions can be inhabited only by an emperor. As the God of Mount Taishan had been given the title Virtuous and Sacred Emperor Equal to Heaven of the Sacred Eastern Mountain in the Song Dynasty, he was qualified to live in a hall of this size.

Tiankuang Hall was of the highest standard in ancient China, as is evident from its roof, which has four slopes, one upper ridge and four sloping ridges. This type of roof, with four slopes and five ridges is called a hip roof. With double eaves added, it becomes a double-eave hip roof, one of the highest ranks of ancient Chinese buildings, reserved exclusively for the main hall of imperial palaces. Today there are only two halls in China with this kind of roof: this one and the Hall of Supreme Harmony of the Imperial Palace in Beijing. Although the Hall of Great Achievements of the Confucius Temple in Qufu City, Shandong, is built to Nine-five dimensions, its roof is

Taishan Archway, the gateway to Mount Taishan

a lower ranking: a double-eave gable and hip roof with four slopes on the lower part, but only two — the front and back — slopes on the upper part, the left and right sides being vertical triangular walls.

The axis of the Temple of Mount Taishan happens to face the middle path for climbing the mountain, and is almost aligned with the summit. Since the Song Dynasty, all memorial arches, towers and pavilions have been built along the axis. The architecture of Mount Taishan unswervingly seeks the idea of order —

consistency, symmetry and balance, which shows not only the molding of nature by culture, but, more importantly, the political needs of Chinese emperors; Mount Taishan had been strongly politicized since the day it became the sacred mountain where emperors went to offer sacrifices to heaven. Even a religious building like the Temple of Mount Taishan inevitably reflected politics.

If the layout of buildings in imperial capitals in ancient China had to follow the principle of spreading out along a central

The First Gate to Heaven spans the pathway. It is the starting point of the pathway up the mountain.

axis, in conformity with the highly centralized feudal culture and rituals, then to stubbornly follow the same principle of architectural construction in a natural environment of undulating mountains and zigzagging mountain paths here on Mount Taishan is a shocking revelation of the unswerving cultural determination of the ancient people.

The statue of the God of Mount Taishan, the Eastern Sacred Mountain, sits erect in the vast Hall of Heavenly Blessing, wearing an imperial crown with nine jade strings, a robe of imperial yellow, and holding a tapering jade tablet engraved with the sun, moon, stars, rivers, seas and mountains. On the beam above the statue is hung a horizontal board bearing an inscription in gold characters "Pei Tian Zuo Zhen" (Maintaining Stability for Heaven) written by the Qing Emperor Kangxi. In this figure, people can see the fusion of divine and imperial power.

The Houzai (Great Virtue Bearing) Gate is the northern gate of the Temple of Mount Taishan. Perhaps because it was the back door to the residence of the so-called Emperor of the Eastern Scared Mountain, people adopted the name commonly used for the rear entrance of imperial palaces in ancient times. In fact, the temple had nothing to do with emperors or empresses. The gate has another name, and it is a good one:

Cool breeze and bright moon were the natural scenery that the ancient Chinese writers longed for. On a cliff west of the trail that winds north of the Ten Thousand Immortals Tower is a two character inscription; the characters for wind and moon have been written with their outside strokes omitted, symbolizing the boundlessness of the view.

Luzhan (Lu Viewing — meaning the State of Lu looking up) Gate. This was an ingenious conception by the designer of the axis, as it stood directly opposite the Zhanlu (Viewing Lu — meaning looking down at the State of Lu) Terrace on the summit. The State of Lu looked up with reverence at Mount Taishan while the sage looked down at the State of Lu; one looking north, the other, south, each of the positioned on the axis — what a culturally and historically rich design!

Pass through the Great Virtue Bearing

The Mid-way Gate to Heaven standing on Huangxian Peak, also known as the Second Gate to Heaven

The Eighteen Mountain Bends from Duisong Mountain to the South Gate to Heaven is the steepest section of the ascent to the summit. ▶

At the top of the Eighteen Mountain Bends stands the South Gate to Heaven, also known as the Third Gate to Heaven, which leads to the summit.

Gate, then the Memorial Archway for Mount Taishan, and slowly climb the slope for a few hundred meters, and you reach the First Gate to Heaven where a notice saying that the stairway to heaven is beneath your feet. And here you start with the first verse of the divine song to heaven.

To enter the First Gate to Heaven is to leave the human world for the divine. To climb up to heaven, a stairway is necessary. The Stairway to Heaven has 6,666 steps, an auspicious number wishing pilgrims good speed and a trouble-free journey. The space between the First Gate to Heaven and the Mid-way Gate to Heaven is the first

heavenly realm, and its "boundless natural beauty" gives pilgrims a first taste of the beautiful land of wonder, as they gradually, unwittingly, leave behind the human world.

The Mid-way Gate to Heaven stands on the ridge of the Huangxian Ridge, where the front fault and the fault at the Mid-way Gate to Heaven intersect. From here to the Cloud Step Bridge is a large level platform, where pilgrims can have a short rest after climbing through the first heavenly realm.

When looking up at Mount Taishan from the foot, you usually "fail to see what Mount Taishan really looks like" because half of the main peak is hidden by the

Huangxian Ridge and the distance is distorted. Only when climbing up the Midway Gate to Heaven, when the open chest and belly of Mount Taishan formed by the fault at the Cloud Step Bridge appears before you, only then is the real appearance of Mount Taishan revealed.

From the Mid-way Gate to Heaven look to the South Gate to Heaven and you feel it is both close and distant, looking so distinct while far, far away.

The South Gate to Heaven stands between the Flying Dragon Rock and Hovering Phoenix Ridge; its red walls and golden tiles set off the blue sky and white clouds, becoming a symbol of paradise. It calls upon people to continue climbing.

Pass through the South Gate to Heaven and go by the Kuaihuo Sanli (Three-*li* Happiness Path), and you see the Cloud Step Bridge. You will also see towering peaks and mountains, hovering clouds, splashing water, thousands of sturdy pines, and overhanging clouds.... Here the divine song to heaven suddenly reaches an exciting crescendo.

The Scaling Ladder to Heaven, comprising three sections of zigzagging paths known as "Eighteen Mountain Bends" has altogether 1,597 steps. The winding path, although less than one kilometer long, is more than 400 meters high, an indication of how steep it is. When pilgrims get to this point, they mostly crawl up on all fours,

completing the last climb in a zigzag course.

Since antiquity the process of ascending Mount Taishan has been a journey of spiritual enlightenment. On rocks along the winding path, climbers from different ages have engraved epigrams expressing their feelings. The Chinese pioneering spirit has encouraged generations after generation, and the magnificent and towering Mount Taishan has become the spiritual summons of this great people.

Yang Xin, a noted aesthetician, set out to climb Mount Taishan for the 28th time at the age of 77. A dozen years earlier, he and his wife had both been diagnosed as having incurable diseases. His wife had departed, while he took up with Mount Taishan and started a new life journey.

Having climbed time and again, he broke through the utmost limits of life, the cancer cells disappeared from his body, and Mount Taishan became the life's destination and spiritual home of Professor Yang. His *Ode to Mount Taishan*, written with great fervor, has been engraved on Mount Taishan, another vivid testimony to the spirit of the mountain.

"Mount Taishan is high but can be climbed, magnificent but amiable; pines and rocks are its bones while clear springs compose its heart; it breathes in the universe, exhales and inhales winds and clouds; it has the sea and sky as its bosom, and bears the soul of Cathay."

At the Summit

Go north from the South Gate to Heaven, turn east, go up the steps, and you reach the Heavenly Street. As the name implies, it is heaven's market. Naturally, neither the emperor of heaven nor the immortals needed to trade goods, and the Heavenly Street was specially established for mortal men. Perhaps since the Qing Dynasty, there have been "a score or so shops" set up on the north side of the street, thus forming the market.

In winter, when temperatures fall below zero at the top of Mount Taishan, the mountain displays its superb beauty under the sunshine. Rime and hoarfrost fall on the rocks, dry twigs, palaces and halls, trees and the Heavenly Street, turning them into ice sculptures.

Soon we come in sight of the summit, the Jade Emperor Peak.

The Jade Emperor Peak, originally called the Heavenly Pillar Peak, was renamed following the building of the Jade Emperor Temple in the Ming Dynasty.

The temple is not large. The main palace consists of three bays with corridors in front and behind. Inside there is a Ming Dynasty bronze statue of the Jade Emperor. This is the place that takes

Shops line the north side of the Heavenly Street, northeast of the South Gate to Heaven.

Hoar frost decorating the summit as in a fairyland

Rock bearing the inscription "The Uppermost Peak" on the summit of Mount Taishan

charge of heaven, earth, gods, all living creatures, men and ghosts, and listens to the earthly emperors praying.

The Summit Rock at the center of the temple courtyard is the summit of Mount Taishan, which is 1,545 meters above sea level. In ancient times, the emperors who came to Mount Taishan to hold mountain worship ceremonies regarded this spot as the most sacred place. Later on, people built the Jade Emperor Temple on the summit and the Summit Rock was buried beneath it. Not until the Ming Dynasty, when an official named Wan Gong moved the Jade Emperor Temple to the north, was the rock exposed and given the protection of a stone barrier.

We can imagine, before the Jade Emperor Temple was built, what people reaching the Summit Rock would feel.

At the moment you stand on the Summit Rock, you can "only feel heaven right above you and nothing else exists." You yourself are the summit now.

Since antiquity, multitudes of tribal chiefs, allied leaders, emperors, scholars, poets and commoners have undergone the long hard ascent to Mount Taishan's summit to experience just one moment of reaching the summit both of the mountain and of life itself.

Perhaps right then, heaven arises in the deep recesses of the pilgrim's soul.

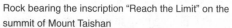

Rock bearing the inscription "Reach the Limit" on the summit of Mount Taishan

Souls Returning to Mount Taishan

The Chinese of antiquity imagined Mount Kunlun not only as the mountain of immortals, gods and heaven but also the Heavenly Emperor's nether world. Beneath the mountain was the dwelling place of all ghosts, in other words, hell.

It was said that when Great Yu was trying to control the flood, he excavated the land at the foot of the Kunlun Grave, as a result digging out a nine-level hell and the torrential Yellow Spring (the netherworld). In fact, the names the ancient Chinese people gave it make apparent Mount Kunlun's double role — both heaven and hell. When they wanted to say the Mount Kunlun was a sacred mountain of heaven, they used the word "mound"; when they wanted to say it was hell, they referred to it as "grave."

In the past, it was thought that Chinese ideas of heaven and hell had been introduced from Buddhism, but this is not the case.

The owner of the Han Tomb at Mawangdui in Changsha, Hunan Province, was buried in 168 BC before Buddhism came to China. The brocade excavated there pictures the owner riding a dragon and ascending to heaven. The

Inscription of Lu Ji's *Song to Mount Taishan,* preserved in the Temple of Mount Taishan

wooden tablets are a letter to the ruler of the underworld, giving a detailed account of the treasures buried with the dead. This demonstrates that more than 2,000 years ago, the idea prevailed that people could go either to heaven or to hell when they died. This idea originated from the belief that after someone dies his soul leaves his body.

What is soul? The ancient Chinese people thought of soul as the substance forming man's spirit, a light gas, similar to cloud or mist. After death, it would leave the body, rise into the air and float.

Then what happens to the substance that forms man's physical body? It would rot and seep into the earth.

To their way of thinking, soul and body should have a home. But where?

Since about 100 BC, two beliefs have been widely held in both the Central Plains and the surrounding land, namely that Chinese people's souls return to Mount Taishan after they die and that Mount Taishan can control ghosts.

During the Eastern Han Dynasty (25-220), iron pledges buried at tombs were often inscribed with the words "Living persons belong to Chang'an; the departed go to Mount Taishan."

Mount Taishan, that is the ancient Mount Kunlun, was taken as the ideal dwelling place for the soul and body.

Early in the Han Dynasty, people even created a song lamenting the inevitability of life's coming to an end, and the inevitable ending of life has constituted a main tragic theme in literature for hundred of years since.

The Netherworld

The mural on the southeast corner of the wall inside Tiankuang Hall portrays the 18 Yamas of the Palace of Darkness standing solemnly on the western bank of the Bridge over the Abyss, bidding farewell to the God of Mount Taishan following his inspection tour of hell.

The place portrayed in this mural corresponds to the layout of the city of Tai'an.

Starting from the First Gate to Heaven following the line of the axis leading to the mountain are the three levels of heaven, symbolized by the three Gates to Heaven. At the Mid-way Gate to Heaven is the West Stream, flowing southwest to the city. On the fault above

The ghost dwelling place in the Haoli Mountain is where the souls of the dead gather, giving rise to the concept of ghost immortals. Therefore this cave in the Haoli Mountain is named Ghost Immortals Cave.

the Black Dragon Pool Waterfall, along the cliff edge, is a white line — the renowned "Borderline between *Yin* and *Yang*" and it is from this borderline that the West Stream falls into the Black Dragon Pool. Clearly, the "Borderline between *Yin* and *Yang*" is the natural dividing line between the netherworld and the real world. Not far from here, the West Stream goes into the city area, forming a torrential river whose name — the Naihe or Abyss River — is a household word in China. But most people think of it as mythical river, very few associate it with Mount Taishan. East of the Abyss River are all houses, prosperous streets and human activity, the world of man. The river is spanned by the Golden Bridge and the Silver Bridge. Descriptions of hell in Chinese folk tales say that once soul and body cross the bridges, there is no returning. Heading west after crossing the river, the land perceptibly gets lower and lower. On this stretch of lowland used to be two hills; one was Sheshou Hill where emperors once held the earth worship as part of the mountain worship ceremony, but it was blasted in the 1950s to make way for the building of Tai'an Railway Station; the other is Haoli Hill, which still remains under a mantle of green pines, but the ancestral temples of kings of hell and ghosts built over dynasties — the 72 departments of Hell — no longer survive.

Great Emperor of the Eastern Sacred Mountain

The God of the Eastern Sacred Mountain, the Great Emperor of Mount Taishan, is the presiding force of the three realms. It is he who consigns to heaven or to hell, according to their vices and virtues before death, all the ghosts assembled by local village, land and town gods.

On the stele, *Chart of the True Form of the Five Sacred Mountains,* are inscribed pictographs of the five sacred mountains and the clearly defined work remits of the gods of the five sacred mountains. The God of Mount Taishan is the most powerful, deciding the life span, job positions and social status of people all over the world.

In the hierarchy of gods in Taoism, Mount Taishan has another title — "True Arbiter of Life and Death."

It is obvious that this title and the scope of his responsibilities originate from the traditional beliefs that "departed souls return to Mount Taishan" and that "Mount Taishan governs ghosts."

The God of Mount Taishan had enormous power, and was directly responsible for mortal man's happiness and station in life, in this world and the next. For this reason, all China, people from the mighty capital to the smallest county town,

Statue of the God of the Eastern Sacred Mountain of Mount Taishan, enshrined in the South Gate to Heaven

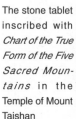

The stone tablet inscribed with *Chart of the True Form of the Five Sacred Mountains* in the Temple of Mount Taishan

would come to the Temple of Mount Taishan, to invite a spirit tablet of the Great Emperor of the Eastern Sacred Mountain to take home and enshrine. In this way, temples to the Eastern Sacred Mountain spread all over the country.

Rebirth

There is some evidence to show that Mount Taishan probably was a sacred place where Chinese ancestors would offer sacrifices to pray for children. Big Heavenly Candle Peak and Lesser Heavenly Candle Peak (also called Ox Heart Rock) at Houshiwu (the Rear Rock Basin), and the Gongbei Rock, which points toward Jade Girl Peak on the summit of Mount Taishan, were male phallic symbols worshipped by Chinese ancestors.

Today, traces of this traditional ceremony of praying for children can still be seen everywhere on Mount Taishan. From the foot of the mountain, along the Stairway to Heaven, all the way up to the mountain summit, we often see grannies or young women burning incense offerings, placing a stone on a stele or tree branch, or tying a strip of red cloth to a branch.

The reason for this is tied up with sounds. *Shi Zi* (stone) has the same pronunciation as another expression meaning "to pick up a child." *Ya Zhi* (putting a stone on a tree branch) sounds the same as "get a child," and *Shuan Zhi* (tying red cloth to a branch) sounds like "to bring up a child." So, in the countryside of Shandong Province, many boys have the pet name "*Shi Zi*" or "*Shuan Zi*," being the babies their grannies and mothers prayed for on Mount Taishan. These

Gongbei Rock on the Sun Watching Peak on the summit

Lesser Heavenly Candle Peak at the Rear Rock Basin

women believe that children reborn from the stones of Mount Taishan have very strong life force and can overcome any hardships. Why? Because the spirit of hundreds of generations of Chinese people is distilled in the rocks and vegetation of Mount Taishan!

A place of heaven, a place of hell, a place where soul and body separate and rejoin — Mount Taishan was believed by Chinese people to be the home mountain — where life is born, returns and is reborn once more.

Once the soul returns to Mount Taishan, it is settled and at peace!

Old woman devoutly tying a strip of red cloth to a tree branch. Is she wishing for a child or blessing?

Stones symbolizing having children or blessing piled up on top of steles

Chapter IV

Mount Taishan and Taoism

Mount Taishan and Living Immortals

Every morning, the peaks on Mount Taishan are awoken by the sound of the bell on top of the mountain. The sound of the bell has lingered here for over a thousand years.

Over the past thousand years, the world has experienced tremendous changes and transformations; dynasties have come and gone, species have become extinct, rivers have changed their courses, cities have sprung up, lives have perished in wars and new lives have been born. Only the bell on top of Mount Taishan keeps sounding, at its same rhythm, day in day out, year after year.

There is hardly a famous mountain in China without associations with Taoism or Buddhism. Mount Taishan, which held a sacred position in state politics, also enjoyed a high status in the world of Taoism. Known as Pengxuan, it occupied second place in the hierarchy of 36 renowned dwellings of immortals across the country. In ancient times, Tai'an was called "Shen Zhou" or "Magic Land," revealing that it was a place of many immortals. There was a saying, in circulation for a long, long time, referring to the city of Ji'nan's large human population and Tai'an's large population of immortals. Even before Taoism was formally created in the 2nd century, many "living immortals" had lived on Mount Taishan. Their high reputations and magic powers made even mighty rulers of millions such as the First Emperor of Qin and Emperor Wu of Han putty in their hands, ready to be

Ten Thousand Immortals Tower

manipulated by them like puppets.

Taoism was based on the theories of scholars from the State of Qi and combined many elements — classic concepts of the Taoist patriarch Laozi, *yin-yang* thinking, the five-element theory, and ideas about immortals. But the mainstream of Taoism was alchemic theory.

The area between the East Sea and Mount Taishan was the place where immortals and alchemists originated. Nie Zheng, a renowned swordsman of the Warring States Period, spent seven years cultivating himself in a cave in Mount Taishan. To revenge his dead father, Nie practiced martial arts while learning to play the *qin* harp. One day, when he got a chance to play for the King of the State of Han, he had a sword hidden in the musical instrument and assassinated the king with it before killing himself by banging his own head against a palace pillar.

During and after the Qin and Han dynasties, immortality alchemists, taking advantage of the emperors' mountain worship ceremonies on Mount Taishan, combined the tactics of state administration and the supernatural arts of self-cultivation, skillfully incorporating their ideas into the ceremony, and transformed Mount Taishan a place famous for cultivating immortality. Indeed it was at the plan of a Ji'nan alchemist that Emperor Wu had the Wenshang sacrificial structure built on the south side

Statues of immortals inside the Ten Thousand Immortals Tower

of Mount Taishan, the first Taoist palace in history. The legendary immortal who met and gave the emperor a pillow was actually a well-known alchemist who was cultivating himself in the heart of the mountain at the time.

The highest goal of Taoists was to give oneself up to austere discipline in order to achieve immortality. For practicing this discipline, they usually chose high or remote mountains. The majestic Mount Taishan with its many sheer peaks and deep caves had long been an ideal place for alchemists. During the Warring States Period, one of them, Huang Boyang, had lived in seclusion in a cave on Luting Mountain north of Mount Taishan, which got the name "Huang Boyang Cave." It was said that An Qisheng, the most famous "living immortal" who lived between the Qin and Han dynasties, stayed in the Celestial Mountain southeast of Mount Taishan. The First Emperor of Qin once requested an audience with him and spent three days talking with him there.

Hermits at Mount Taishan

Beside those "living immortals", many others from diverse backgrounds also stayed on Mount Taishan for religious self-discipline. They were well versed in astronomy and geography, military tactics and state administration. Whenever the emperor encountered difficulties, he would send for them to give advice.

Loujing Cave, to the northwest of Mount Taishan, received its name from a minister of the Han Dynasty who once hid here in seclusion. Lou Jing, an alchemist of great resource, made three suggestions to Liu Bang, founder of the Han Dynasty (r. 206-195 BC): to make Chang'an the Han capital; to adopt the policy of pacification through marriage with the powerful nomadic tribe of Xiongnu; and to relocate 100,000 people, mostly offspring of former Shandong princes and prominent families, away to the Guanzhong region near the capital city, so as to weaken the forces of the old nobility.

Surrounding the Loujing Cave are precipitous peaks and deep gullies. There are said to be 72 caves in the mountain.

The Virtuous King Mausoleum on the Five Peak Mountain, where six Ming princes cultivated themselves and were buried. (Picture courtesy of Changqing District Publicity Department)

102

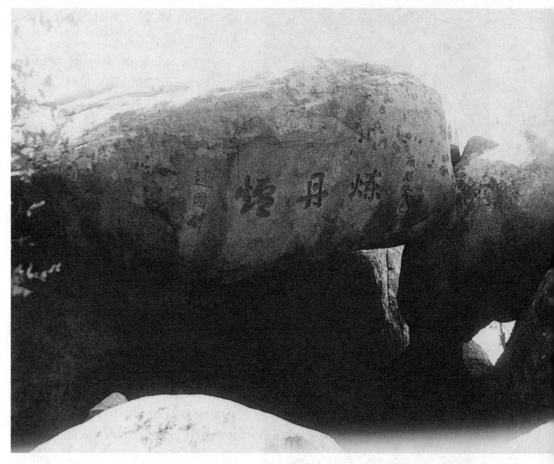

Rock on Mount Culai where the 10th century hermit Chen Tuan made pills of immortality (from *Xintai Culture*)

This one is large enough to accommodate several hundred people. Before Lou Jing, it had also been a shelter for Fan Li, who assisted Gou Jian (King of the State of Yue) in defeating the State of Wu in the 5th century BC, and Zhang Liang, a military counselor to Liu Bang. In the past, stone statues of the three were enshrined in the cave.

Facing the Loujing Cave stands the Five Peak Mountain, one of the birthplaces of Taoism. According to the stele inscriptions, in the 16th and 17th centuries, six princes of the Ming court stayed in the mountain for religious self-discipline, and all were buried here after their death. Even princesses came here to cultivate themselves.

From all the foregoing, it can be concluded that the sacred Mount Taishan may indeed be an ideal place for Chinese and overseas *qigong* practitioners who believe in the theory that man is an integral part of nature.

Rubbing of Culai Mount cliff inscription the "Solitary Graceful Peak", allegedly by Li Bai (from *Xintai Culture*)

ley in the Mount Culai, southeast of Mount Taishan.

At the site of the famous 13th century Ersheng Taoist Temple is a round grave built of stone slabs, under which is a rectangular stone hut. The design is obviously based on the ancient Chinese belief that the heaven is round and the earth is square. The hut may be a so-called "grave for the living." When a Taoist stayed secluded in the hut meditating for a fixed period, the door would be blocked with a huge stone slab, leaving only one opening on the southeast corner for people to send in essential food and water.

According to legend, Mount Culai was where the renowned Tang Dynasty "six hermits of bamboos and streams" stayed. In ancient times, the temperature in northern China was higher than it is now and the mountain landscape was cloaked with luxuriant bamboo forests. The secluded mountain scenery drew to it the poet Li Bai and five other recluses, who would drink liquor and compose poems by the murmuring streams, pick herbs to make pills of immortality in the valleys, and look for immortals in the luxuriant bamboo forests. They rose as the birds began their dawn chorus, and slept when animals returned their dens at dusk, leading a life of blissful happiness, free from care and worry.

Primitive Taoist philosophy held that people should try to maintain the simple state before their minds became perturbed with various desires, and live a natural, harmonious life, impervious to any external attack or disturbance. Chao Fu, a hermit of antiquity, was said to be the first to practice such philosophy in a val-

Li Bai's Hunt for Immortals

Li Bai (701-762), the poet and Taoist layman, called himself a relegated immortal. He described himself as "loving to roam in the five sacred mountains, no matter how far, and seeking immortals all my life."

In 742, in the enchanting month of April, Li Bai began his trip in search of immortals on Mount Taishan, following the same route Emperor Xuanzong had taken. The poet set out in the morning, having supped liquor at Queen Mother Pond, a pond named after the legendary Taoist Queen Mother of the Western Heavens. As he kept stopping on route to take in the wonderful scenery, he did not reach the South Gate to Heaven until dusk. Standing on the summit and looking back the way he had come, he saw dark clouds and lightening accompanied by rumbles of thunder. In the distance loomed the Gold and Silver Terrace of Penglai, the fairly island on the East Sea. Feeling carefree and relaxed, the poet could not help crying loudly to the vast sky. As the breeze lifted his garment, he felt his vision expand so far as to embrace heaven and earth; the universe became so tiny that the worldly

The poet Li Bai

struggle for rank, fame and fortune no longer counted for much.

At night, Li Bai took his *qin* and played it in clear moonlight on the summit. When he raised his head, he saw the Milky Way running over and the stars twinkling so near, as easily reachable as the gourds on the courtyard shed.

Before dawn, the poet climbed onto the Sun Viewing Peak. He reached out and tried to raise the curtain of clouds, feeling like he could jump up and float on the cloud sea.

He did not find the renowned alche-

Stele in the Yaocan Pavilion courtyard with a poem by Li Bai on his ascent of Mount Taishan

mist An Qisheng, but Li Bai did encounter some young Taoist nuns who gave him a cup made from Mount Taishan jade. The fairies were possibly nuns from the Jade Maiden Temple, which was known for its very influential abbess, who often traveled between Mount Taishan and Chang'an and kept in close touch with eminent people in the capital. Liu Yuxi (772-840), another great poet of the Tang Dynasty, wrote a poem for her, praising her "rare elegance and nobility." Inscriptions by the abbess can still be seen on the cliffs behind the Ten Thousand Immortals Tower.

The Free-wheeling Immortal Lu Dongbin

The Ten Thousand Immortals Tower brings us to the subject of Lu Dongbin, who lived in the ninth century and is reputed to be one of the eight Taoist immortals. It is said that when Lu visited Mount Taishan, he dallied with a local girl named White Peony who later gave birth to a boy, Bai Shilang. The boy never met his irresponsible father who had moved on. When he grew up, the boy swore to have his revenge on all immortals. One day, when he heard that Lu Dongbin had come to Mount Taishan, he followed him with a magic gourd, in which he kept all the immortals he managed to catch, as a result it was said to contain a great number of immortals inside. When he encountered his father, the boy was so nervous that he dropped the gourd on the ground, where it smashed, releasing all the immortals trapped within, thus making the place full of immortal spirits. Later, the Ten Thousand Immortals Tower was built on the site.

Two other sites on Mount Taishan are also associated with Lu. One is the Queen Mother Pond. Secreted away to the east of the pond is a cave, on the walls of which Lu himself inscribed a poem. Behind the pond lies a hall in memory of the famous Taoist. The other site is also a cave, by the Residence of the Female Deity at Houshiwu (the Rear Rock Basin).

The cave where Lu Dongbin once lived

Hall in memory of Lu Dongbin

Cave inscriptions said to be Lu Dongbin's calligraphy

The interesting thing is that the two places associated with Lu Dongbin are both close to the residences of female deities and Taoist nuns. This also reflects Lu's dual personality, which was different from what was expected of a decent Confucian scholar and a noble man. He lived an unconventional life, but was true to himself. His conduct revealed the discontent of Chinese scholars toward the Confucian moral rules that had bound them for centuries and their instinct to evade the heavy moral burdens on them. This explains why the dissolute immortal Lu Dongbin has been a favorite of the common people and a certain number of demoralized scholars down the ages.

Queen Mother Pond

On the south slope of Mount Taishan lies an old Taoist temple, Qunyu Nunnery. It derives its alternative name, Queen Mother Pond, from the pond inside the courtyard. The temple accommodated the great poets Cao Zhi (192-232) and Li Bai (701-762) who put their beautiful experiences here into poetry.

Mount Taishan was always a place of relaxation for disappointed scholars who were dissatisfied with reality, but still hoped to find some way out.

Cao Zhi, a prince from the State of Wei, visited the Queen Mother Pond in a miserable plight. Seeing the nuns living at ease there, Cao felt all the more sad at the terrible strife between his power-hungry brothers. Imagining the immortals were beckoning to him from the clouds, he sprang up as light as a bird, and found himself riding auspicious clouds and flying to the top of Mount Taishan. In the heaven he saw majestic palaces, and trees of crystal jade lining the roads. Looking down at the five sacred mountains on earth, Cao came to realize that worldly life was merely a temporary staging post. He sighed deeply, "I am nothing more than a man of Taishan."

Today, the Queen Mother Pond has become the Kundao Nunnery, with nuns from all parts of the country. Taoist believers at home and abroad all regard this place as the ancestral temple of the Queen Mother of the Western Heavens. The newly erected benefaction stele records the names of Chinese and overseas Taoist groups and pilgrims who made donations for the restoration of the complex.

Queen Mother Pond

Cao Zhi's poem in praise of Mount Taishan, in the Temple of Mount Taishan

Statue of the Queen Mother of the Western Heavens enshrined at the temple known as Queen Mother Pond

The hall where the Queen Mother of the Western Heavens is enshrined

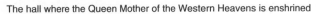

Emperors and Taoist Mount Taishan

In the Tang Dynasty, the Queen Mother Pond was just a part of the Temple of Mount Taishan. Following centuries of development after Taoism was formally established in the 2nd century, the "Original Divinity" was made the supreme deity of Taoism. Since the ruler of the Tang court was surnamed Li, they honored Li Er, (Laozi and founder of Taoist thought) as the "Supreme Monarch" replacing the Original Divinity as the highest deity of Taoism. Li Yuan, Emperor Gaozu and founder of the Tang Dynasty, announced the order of China's three popular religions as: first Taoism, second Confucianism and third Buddhism.

Emperor Gaozong further upgraded Laozi to the status of "Supreme Xuanyuan Emperor" and had a hall built in the Temple of Mount Taishan to enshrine him.

The Double Stone Stele now standing in the temple was first placed in the above-mentioned Supreme Monarch Hall. It was built by Guo Xingzhen, a Taoist priest sent by Emperor Gaozong and Empress Wu Zetian to perform a Taoist ritual for departed souls and build statues on Mount Taishan. Guo came to the mountain as a royal representative five years earlier than the actual trip made by the emperor and empress themselves. The stele bears 24 items of inscriptions; these record the actions, over

143 years, of six Tang Emperors (Gaozong, Zhongzong, Ruizong, Xuanzong, Daizong and Dezong) who sent priests to perform Taoist rituals and erect statues in the temple.

The Maoshan Sect, a Taoist school created in the 5th century, standardized the worship of the five sacred mountains during the Tang Dynasty. In the year 727, Emperor Xuanzong accepted the advice of Sima Chengzhen, the 12th master of the Maoshan Sect, and issued an edict that a temple be built on each of the five sacred mountains. The five mountains thus became Taoist abodes and the mountain gods became the supreme heads of all Taoist deities.

The Temple of Mount Taishan, with various names during the Tang, Song and Ming dynasties were all special places for the royal families to perform Taoist rituals. Often, Taoist priests or eunuchs came here from the capital to perform Taoist services and pray for peace and longevity for the emperor, concubines, princes and princesses.

From the Tang Dynasty on, Taoists

Former site of the hall where Laozi was enshrined, on the western side of Queen Mother Pond

played a major role in staging imperial mountain worship ceremonies on Mount Taishan. Records show that when the large procession of the Tang Emperor Taizong came as far as Luoyang on its way to the sacred mountain, a comet appeared. All the Taoist Xue Yi had to say was "I'm afraid it's not proper to conduct the ceremony" and the emperor stopped and returned home. When Emperor Gaozong was about to set off to Mount Taishan, relentless rain was falling, but after the prayers from the Taoist priest Liu Daohe, the skies cleared and the procession got under way.

A noteworthy phenomenon in Chinese Taoism history is that compilations of Taoist classics at the monarch's order were all associated with Mount Taishan. To be more accurate, large-scale compilation organized by the central government was an integral part of the mountain worship ceremony. The *Kaiyuan Baozang, (Treasure Writings of Kaiyuan)*, the first large Taoist classic in China, destroyed during war in the 19th century, was completed when Emperor Xuanzong conducted the mountain worship ceremony on Mount Taishan. After the Song Emperor Zhenzong's epic mountain worship event here, he ordered Wang Qinruo, who fabricated the so-called "heavenly instructions," to take charge of the compilation of the *Da Song Tiangong Baozang (Great Song Treasure Writings from the Heavenly Palace)*. Zhang Junfang

condensed the essence of this work into one smaller volume in which he placed Mount Taishan second among the 36 Taoist dwelling places and listed all the gods on the mountain into Taoist deities.

The Taoist fervor of the Song court was no less than their Tang counterparts. After Emperor Zhenzong converted into Taoist temples those palaces where previous monarchs had stayed when they came to Mount Taishan, one of his descendents, Emperor Huizong (r. 1101-1125) proclaimed himself patriarch of Taoism, saying that he was the eldest son of the God of Eternity from Heaven and had been sent from heaven to be in charge of the world. He even went a step further and ordered that a palace be built in every prefecture right across China to enshrine tablets to the God of Eternity. With this ridiculous self-deception and self-flattery, the construction of Taoist temples on Mount Taishan reached an unprecedented scale.

In Qin and Han dynasties, the worship ceremonies at Mount Taishan, alchemists played the role of counselors, but in the Tang and Song ceremonies Taoists arranged the events. Since Taoism dominated the state ceremony, it naturally became the major religion on Mount Taishan. The magnificent setting of the axis ascending the mountain from foot to summit on the south slope has made it a showplace and stronghold of Taoism.

Taoist Design of Mount Taishan

Temple of Lord Guan in front of the First Gate to Heaven

Taoism implemented on Mount Taishan a complete and systematic cultural design in conformity with its philosophy.

First, the two ascending routes of the north and the east slopes were dropped, since they did not comply with the Chinese political tradition of "the monarch always facing south." Second, the designers took clever advantage of the three natural faults on the south slope to create the three levels of heaven. Third, they had a central ascending path built along the alignment of the valley, which was in perfect conformity to Chinese political and cultural needs. The central axis intensified the already fixed and symmetrical image of Mount Taishan, and the scene of man climbing northward up the south-facing mountain put Mount Taishan's supremacy into further relief and suited the Chinese people's reverence for heaven.

Just imagine: climbing the mountain, step after step, peaks and ridges on either side rising higher and higher, at intervals encountering a steep flight of steps ahead, naturally, people's hearts would fill with a sense of reverence, longing and mystery. Then, with every higher fault reached, is the great satisfaction of attaining a "higher level of heaven."

Along the axis, Taoist temples, pavil-

Statue of Lord Guan

113

Flying Cloud Tower spanning the roadway, linking the east and west courtyards of the Red Gate Palace

ions and archways have transformed a natural mountain into one replete with religious and cultural atmosphere. Of all the manmade structures, the Stairway to Heaven below the South Gate to Heaven and the Mokong Pavilion can be seen as the final flourishes.

The last section of the Eighteen Mountain Bends originally went east and then turned to the bell tower of the Bixia (Azure Cloud) Temple. The design utilized the natural alignment of the valley, shortened the final distance to the summit and mitigated the angle of the final climb. In terms of efficiency, it was a good choice.

But the efficiency principle came under challenge from the Yuan Dynasty Taoist Zhang Zhichun. At his insistence, the original detour was straightened out, and the last several-hundred-meter section was diverted directly to the narrow pass between Flying Dragon Rock and Hovering Phoenix Ridge. Though this made the ascent more difficult, it intensified the mental and physical experience, bringing the divine song to heaven ascent to a real climax. Still not content, Zhang had the modest Mokong Pavilion the end point of the Stairway to Heaven, creating a symbolic entrance to heaven. It is the final goal for the many who dare test their courage and physical strength to finish the 6,666-step journey.

Zhang reportedly brought many lives back from death through his consummate medical skills. The design of the South Gate to Heaven may be another of his miracles.

Twin Tiger Temple by the Mid-way Gate to Heaven, built specially to protect the mountain from tigers

In line with the ancient belief that "Departed souls return to Mount Taishan" and that "Mount Taishan governs ghosts," the ancient Chinese took advantage of the unique terrain to reproduce on Mount Taishan a complete universe, comprising paradise above, a worldly land in the middle and the netherworld below.

More importantly, Taoism invested the God of Mount Taishan with dual functions.

As the god of the great mountain in

Doumu (Mother of the Big Dipper) Temple, north of the Ten Thousand Immortals Tower, built to worship the Mother of the Big Dipper

The early 19th century Immortal Dreaming Niche, perched half way up the mountain

the east, the God of Mount Taishan was originally in charge of life and spring, because the ancient Chinese believed that the course of the seasons started from the east and that every living thing originated from here.

But, since they also regarded the mountain as the meeting point of *yin* and *yang*, or the netherworld and the human world, they divided the functions of the God of Mount Taishan into two: the one in charge of life and spring was called Emperor of Greenery and enshrined in a temple on the summit; and the other "in charge of ghosts" was called "Emperor of the East Sacred Mountain" and enshrined in the Hall of Heavenly Blessing in the Temple of Mountain Taishan at the foot.

Humans are born with a longing for life and a fear of death; therefore, they pay great attention to death and the afterlife, worshipping the Emperor of the East Sacred Mountain more than the Emperor of Greenery, and demonstrating that, for ordinary Chinese, fear is more effective than hope in inspiring religious devotion.

All in all, Taoism's greatest contribution was the Goddess of Mount Taishan with the mission to deliver all from worldly sufferings and fears.

Her universal love won her the overwhelming support of the masses, who placed the goddess way above all other gods revered by Taoism and made her the true dominant spirit of Mount Taishan.

Chapter V

Mount Taishan Deities

Bixia Temple

The Bixia (Azure Cloud) Temple is a complex of grand buildings set among high mountains, located on the top of Mount Taishan. When looked up at from the Heavenly Street, the temple is surrounded by clouds, like the heavenly residence of the Yuanjun (Supreme Monarch) Goddess; if looked down on from the summit, its palaces and halls hide between the peaks.

The temple consists of two courtyards. The main hall has five bays, nine ridges, a gable and hip roof and 360 runs of curved tiles, symbolizing the number of days in a year by the lunar calendar. Because the of the fog and rain on the high mountain, wood is vulnerable to decay, and tiles can easily wrecked by the strong winds, therefore the tiles and other parts of the temple were made of iron. In the early Qing Dynasty the iron tiles were replaced with bronze tiles. In the front courtyard of the main hall stands the Fragrance Pavilion dating from the Ming Dynasty. In the late Ming, Li Zicheng's peasant rebellion army, seeing the gilded bronze pavilion, thought it was real gold and made off with it to the bottom of the mountain. When they discovered it was bronze, they scraped off the gold and discarded the pavilion at the Lingying Palace of the Lower Temple of Yuanjun. Later, it was moved to the Temple of Mount Taishan.

It can be imagined how impressive a temple fair held in a bronze-tile and gold-plated pavilion would be!

In terms of scale and materials, the Bixia Temple stands out from all the structures at the top of Mount Taishan. One of the six wonders on the mountaintop, the divine glow emerges among the clouds and fog outside the Sacred Gate of the temple. When the light appears, a huge aureole hangs on the eave corner of the temple like a rainbow. In the past, people were not familiar with refraction; they thought it was a sacred mystery, that it was the Goddess Bixia Yuanjun showing her presence; therefore, when the divine glow emerged, the crowds would get excited. Anyone whom this light shone upon would feel supremely lucky.

Aureole glowing over the Bixia Temple

118

Bixia Temple on top of Mount Taishan

History of the Goddess of Mount Taishan

Since the 1980s, stone figures of naked pregnant women have been found among the early Neolithic cultural relics unearthed in North China. These prehistoric Chinese "Venuses" had many functions and responsibilities, being family protection goddess, earth mother goddess and fertility goddess. In particular, the large primitive altar and goddess temple excavated along with them have brought home to us matriarchal society's primitive custom of knowing only the mother but not the father, causing us to appreciate the urgent desire of our ancestors' prayers for fecundity.

On Mount Moshan to the north of Mount Taishan there was a strange circle stone structure. It is said that someone had heard during one night singing on the mountain of the work song usually sung when shifting heavy things. In the morning it was discovered that huge rocks had been piled into a circle. It is also said that five goddesses had been seen piling up the huge rocks at night, so this mysterious stone circle was also called the "Stone Circle of Five Goddesses."

Was this sacrificial altar of the Goddess of Mount Taishan?

It is said that in the year Emperor Zhenzong of Song performed the moun-

Statue of the goddess Bixia Yuanjun

tain worship ceremony on Mount Taishan, someone washing his hands in a small pool on the mountaintop chanced to find a stone sculpture of a goddess; therefore, the emperor issued orders to build the Temple of Uncovering the Truth on the spot. At that time there was no Bixia Yuanjun goddess, and people simply called the statue the Jade Girl. In fact, early in the Tang Dynasty, on Mount Taishan there had been Yuanjun Goddess temples run by Taoist nuns. The Tang Dynasty poet Liu Yuxi (772-842) wrote a poem to the Taoist Zhang Lianshi on the latter's return to

Mount Taishan, including the line "You have served the Yuanjun Goddess in green mountains for a long time." Yuanjun is the highest title accorded to female deities in Taoism. By the Ming Dynasty, the Goddess of Mount Taishan had the beautiful and respectful title of Bixia Yuanjun (Supreme Monarch of Azure Cloud). However, ordinary people seem to prefer calling her "Mount Taishan Granny."

"Mount Taishan Granny, you are so powerful, please protect my kind-hearted daughter's beauty. I'm kowtowing to you, Granny, and you can't make things more difficult for me. I climb the high mountain once a year to bring you clothes...."

This is a prayer chanted by an 80-year-

Where the Jade Girl cultivated the Way of Perfection

old grandmother whose daughter had lost all her hair because of a rare disease. She had seen many doctors without result. The old woman climbs Mount Taishan every year to pray to the goddess to make her daughter's hair grow back.

Bixia Yuanjun Temple on the Rear Rock Basin

123

The characters for "baldachin" carved on a cliff face, a reference to the baldachin shape of Jade Girl Mountain

Yellow Flower Cave, situated in front of the Yaoguan Terrace on Jade Girl Mountain, said to be where the Jade Girl cultivated the Way and became an immortal

Rear Rock Basin in winter

Cult of the Goddess

The cult of the Bixia Yuanjun goddess really began to get serious from the Ming Dynasty onwards.

From a historical perspective, once patriarchal society replaced matriarchal society, the goddesses of primitive worship retreated from the stage of history. As with the secular world, the world of religion was dominated by men. However, at the beginning of the Ming Dynasty, its first Emperor Zhu Yuanzhang took away the imperial title of the God of Mount Taishan, and stopped mountain worship ceremonies, so putting an end to the emperors' previous monopolization of Mount Taishan and returning it to the people. The Goddess of Mount Taishan made a sudden return to the belief system of people in northern China. Combining all the compassion and magic of primitive fertility goddesses, Taoist immortals and Buddhist Guanyin, she descended to the sky of

The "stop-over" dwelling for the goddess Bixia Yuanjun

For hundreds of years, Bixia Yuanjun Temple has attracted throngs of worshippers.

North China and became the highest divinity in northern people's beliefs. A Ming Dynasty novel describes her thus: "She guards Mount Taishan, resides in the South Sea, dispels eight adversities, and eliminates three disasters; she is sympathetic, saves people from miseries; responds to people's requests; she is sacred and very effective." She was extolled to such an extent that people become confused whether she is the Bodhisattva of the South Sea or the Bixia Yuanjun Goddess of Mount Taishan.

With the opening up of the Grand Canal between Hangzhou and Beijing, water transportation boomed and the Bixia Yuanjun goddess was also entitled "Blessing and Virtue Goddess Who Forever Protects the Canal," similar to the Heavenly Queen of Mazu worshipped by fishermen along the South China coast. Then the Ming Dynasty Emperor Chongzhen (r. 1628-1644) conferred upon Mazu the title of Bixia Yuanjun. Consequently, on both banks of the canal, every county built stop-

over palaces for the goddess and some counties had as many as eight. Statistics show that almost every one of China's 2,000 counties had a Yuanjun temple.

Beijing also had five temples dedicated to the goddess, namely the Golden Summit, Eastern Summit, Western Summit, Southern Summit and Northern Summit. The Golden Summit Temple on Mount Miaofeng had the most worshippers and it was packed with people at every Golden Summit Temple fair held on the first day of the 4th lunar month. It is said that the Qing Empress Dowager Cixi (1835-1908) came here and burned the first incense to pray for the health of her son Emperor Tongzhi (r. 1862-1874) who had smallpox.

During the Ming Dynasty, when the number of pilgrims from all over China coming to worship Bixia Yuanjun on Mount Taishan reached a million, the local government of Tai'an imposed an incense tax, making it impossible for many poor people to go to the summit to offer

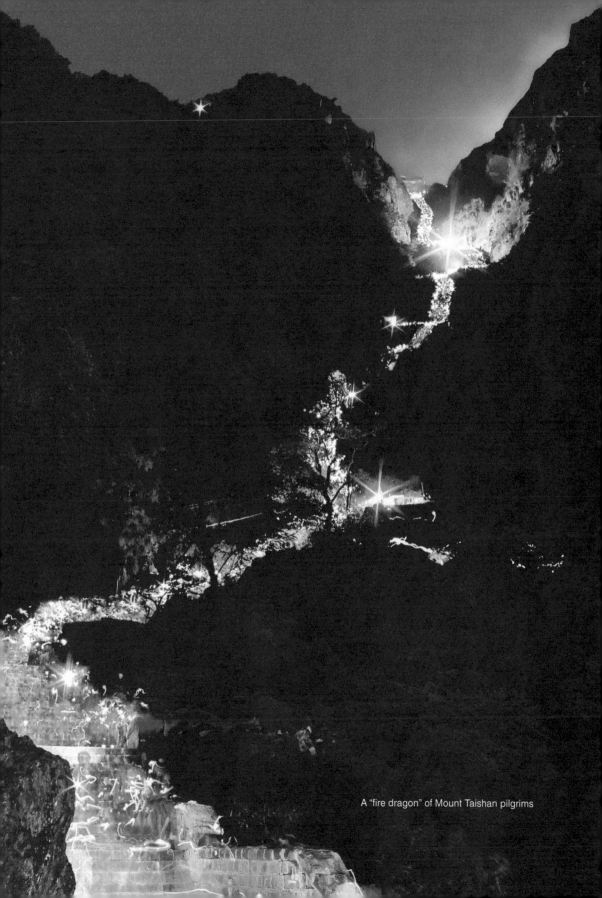

A "fire dragon" of Mount Taishan pilgrims

Lighting incense and praying

incense. Therefore, devout but poor worshippers adopted a natural rock at the Red Gate of the entrance of Mount Taishan as the reincarnation of Mount Taishan Granny. The rock was called "Lesser Mount Taishan." On the 18th day of the 4th lunar month, the birthday of Bixia Yuanjun, the "Lesser Mount Taishan" is visited by multitudes of worshippers who buy paper money and gold or silver paper ingots to burn before the rock.

In the Ming Dynasty, the cult of Bixia Yuanjun in northern China reached a new peak, with thousands upon thousands of pilgrims going to Mount Taishan in scenes comparable to the imperial mountain worship ceremonies of the past. The Ming Dynasty writer Zhang Dai (1597-1676) saw the pilgrims, going up or coming down the mountain, all loudly chanting Amitabha to the rhythmic beat of gongs, their voices stirring the whole mountain. Each carried a "Respecting Yuanjun Goddess" lantern and those lantern lights wound their way for 20 kilometers, light-

ing up the whole mountain as if every star in the sky had fallen into the valleys of Mount Taishan!

In 1594 (the 22nd year of the reign period of Emperor Wanli of Ming), Prime Minister Wang Xijue recorded what he had seen on the *Stele of the Bixia Yuanjun Temple Palace on the East Sacred Mountain:* "Over the vast land of Qi and Lu, the line of worshippers murmuring Amitabha extended several thousand kilometers. Their feet were blistered, their walking sticks broken, but they still moved on. I asked them what they were doing. They said they were going to pray to the Bixia Yuanjun Goddess. When I asked them what they wanted they told me she could satisfy any wish they had. Poor people wanted to become rich; sick people wanted to get well; farmers wanted good harvests; merchants wanted to make their fortune; people who wished for longevity asked for longer life; people without descendents asked for grandchildren; sons made wishes about their parents; younger brothers made wishes for older brothers; and close friends and relatives all made wishes for each other. And that the goddess sincerely promised to grant all wishes and made them come true.

People prayed to her about natural disasters and hardships in their life. When classical religion colluded with the autocratic, corrupt politics that savagely oppressed common people and became more and more remote from them, those poor people who were in desperate need of compassion took the kind-hearted, brave and clever goddess as their loving mother who brought solace to their wretched souls. In folk stories, this goddess fights against the Jade Emperor, Buddha, the dragon king and with demons and devils; keeps good weather for the crops and promises good harvests; punishes the bad and protects the weak; grants children and cures diseases; and keeps women and children healthy....

In 1580, the governor of Shandong Province He Qiming ascended to the summit of Mount Taishan, seeing pilgrims from all over China wailing and kowtowing to the statue of Bixia Yuanjun, as if they were returning to their mother's bosom after experiencing all the suffering in the world. This governor was shocked at how the ordinary people hated their real life. He was afraid. Therefore, he ordered the magistrate of Tai'an to inform all worshippers that they should transfer to the emperor the dedication and piety they showed Bixia Yuanjun. This is an accurate reflection of the political weakness of the late Ming Dynasty.

By contrast, in the third golden age of Chinese feudal society in the 17th and 18th centuries, the flourishing reigns of the Qing emperors Kangxi and Qianlong,

rather than discouraging worship of the goddess, actually encouraged it. During the reign of Emperor Kangxi, the building of stop-over palaces to the goddess reached a peak. Even the epigraph to the *Record of Bixia Yuanjun Temples* in Taixing County, Jiangsu, says, "Building stop-over palaces for the goddess Bixia Yuanjun is beneficial to national politics and religion." Emperor Qianglong himself wrote for the "Stele of Record of Renovating the Temple of Bixia Yuanjun". He believed that "State sacrifices to the God of Mount Taishan may appear different from millions of commoners offering sacrifices to Bixia Yuanjun, but actually they are the same." They were like the *yin* and *yang* of the universe; the Great Emperor of East Sacred Mountain sitting in the Temple of Mount Taishan, wearing a tasseled crown and holding a tapering jade tablet, was actually the same being as the goddess Bixia Yuanjun sitting in the Bixia Temple, wearing women's clothes and hairpins. Like *yin* and *yang* in Taoism, both national politics and folk religion aim to make the country stable and the people peaceful. Emperor Qianlong was of the view that since the sacrifices for the God of Mount Taishan were the exclusive preserve of the state, common people should devote their piety to the goddess Bixia Yuanjun.

The idea that gods exist if you believe

and that they will manifest themselves if you worship has been widely believed by Chinese people for a long time. Folk gods become objects of veneration precisely because they are very close to people's lives, suited to their taste, and do not entail complicated rituals and recital of scriptures.

On Goddess Yuanjun's birthday, happiness permeates the entire land of Shandong. Pilgrims holding various sacrifices wind up all the way to Mount Taishan. The most conspicuous are the "ten thousand people umbrellas" made of colorful cloth stripes, signed with the names of thousands of worshippers and bearing their sentiments, who may not be present but whose regard is symbolized by the umbrellas. If a worshipper comes with a "ten-thousand-people umbrella," he represents ten thousand people.

As times change, worshippers' wishes change too. Besides the common requests for health, longevity and family security, they add new requests reflecting today's life, such as job promotion and family harmony.

Foreign scholars consider that the Chinese attitude toward religion is a pragmatic one, without any deep, pious feelings; that they are brilliant at exploiting and transforming all manner of religious resources, twisting and re-shaping them in search of fame and wealth, even playing with or rejecting them as their interests and needs dictate.

In the mid-1960s, as the economy in Taiwan took off, there was a very interesting phenomenon: Christianity declined gradually while folk religion grew stronger by the day. Scholars analyzed the phenomenon thus: Christianity emphasizes "original sin" and "salvation," it cannot guarantee a business will make money, whereas the folk gods promise everything. They are more suited to the adaptable small family business economy. Since the 1980s, this social phenomenon has been repeated in the full in the mainland, too. The renaissance of local religion does reflect a practical attitude toward religion; in fact, in Chinese folk culture, various religious norms can be easily discarded. This is a perfect illustration of the survival wisdom and vitality of the Chinese people who struggle in a constrained living space. They simply ask for what they really need.

Given the nature of their belief culture, Chinese people feel free to create their own gods. Consequently, one of the main features of folk religion is polytheism and each god has specific duties. Of the religious activities of ordinary Chinese, the most clearly utilitarian aspect is the conduct shown when praying to those gods.

However, if you look beyond the surface, look into the belief the Chinese have in such "omnipotent gods" as the Jade Emperor, Bodhisattva and the Supreme Monarch of Azure Cloud, you will find the deep, non-utilitarian religious affection that is still the spiritual support of Chinese people's beliefs.

Karl Marx once remarked that the ideology of the ruling class was the ruling thought. Though folk religion is the truest reflection of people's minds, it shared the same values as governing officialdom, i.e., "ruling the world with morality." This attitude is the intrinsic reason why the Chinese accept different religious beliefs without making clear-cut distinctions between them. To their eyes, the difference between gods and humans lies in the gods'

ability to protect the weak, punish the evil and reward the good — this is what ordinary people understand by the word "morality." A Westerner or a theologian cannot fathom how Chinese can pick and mix from different religions, sometimes even contradictory teachings. It is a big puzzle to them how pious Chinese will burn incense in any temple and kowtow to any god. But if they went below the surface, disregarding all the trappings and the gods' external appearance, what they would find is the real implication of the people's belief system, namely "virtue and morality."

Ordinary people's beliefs and official ideology share another article of faith,

Red loops around the bronze lions on balustrade posts, tied there as prayers for blessing by people ascending Mount Taishan

namely that "The country is most important." Many worshippers first pray for the peace of the nation and everybody in it before praying for individual and family blessings.

Going into things further, another interesting phenomenon emerges, namely that, as you go up from the Queen Mother Pond all the way to the Bixia Temple, all the gods in the temples are female — the Queen Mother, the Nine-lotus Bodhisattva, the Bodhisattva of Wisdom, Mother of the Big Dipper, Goddess of Mercy, the Three Great Scholars and the Goddess Bixia Yuanjun. In the Three Scholar Palace, two deities that are elsewhere depicted as males — the Bodhisattva of Wisdom and the Bodhisattva of Universal Benevolence — have here been obliged to change their sex and wear bound-feet shoes!

In this world ruled by goddesses, Bixia Yuanjun deserves the title Queen of Mount Taishan. At the end of a long, 17th century novel entitled *Random Notes on Taowu,* the goddess sits in final judgment on peoples' kindness and enmity, good conduct and bad. The writer depicts Bixia Yuanjun as a goddess of Taoism, the Buddhism Goddess of Mercy and all the more like the Holy Mother of Christianity. Yuanjun had become the highest goddess, overriding the world, surpassing the three religions (Confucianism, Taoism and Buddhism). The sacred altar of the final judgment was built on the emperors' sacrificial altar on Mount Taishan. Mount Taishan, an imperial mountain since the beginning of time, was for ordinary people purely and simply the place where rites to Bixia Yuanjun were performed. So, for centuries, many worshippers were aware only of the name Mountain Granny, not Mount Taishan.

Originally, Taoists picked out Bixia Yuanjun from all the other folk gods to set against the Goddess of Mercy in Buddhism. Her duties were originally confined to curing sickness (particularly eye diseases and smallpox) and granting children. Her image was simply that of a goddess protecting the lives and interests of women and children.

This humbly-born goddess could not be entered on the formal regular register of gods, on a par with heavenly emperors or kings. However, the status of a god depends on what people believe, not on its ranking in some bureaucratic grouping of gods. The faithful vote with their incense! Bixia Yuanjun has no noble family background or conspicuous powers, no superweapons or fantastic magic arts. Her allpowerful status was won by her loving and compassionate heart, her awareness of ordinary people, her sympathy for their suffering and her spirit of saving the world and men. By contrast, the high-ranking gods of the Taoist hierarchy were too keen on ruling, with very little idea of serving their worshippers and rescuing them from adversity. Therefore, the Temple of the Jade Emperor next to the Bixia Temple has few worshippers, and the three highest-ranking Buddhas do not even have temples on the axis. Even the God of Mount Taishan has been ignored by people. At the end of the day, orthodox Taoism, the Taoism that flourished in the Tang and Song dynasties and specially served the royal family and officialdom, has to survive on the worship of the goddess Bixia Yuanjun. Does this not provide food for thought? The ancient maxims "who wins the hearts and minds of the people wins the world," and "the water that floats the boat can also overturn it" surely apply to Taoist Mount Taishan beliefs as well as they do to earthly politics!

Taoist priests in Robes of Longevity offering sacrifices and praying at the Bixia Temple

Mount Taishan Rock of Protection

Mount Taishan by no means embodies only the feminine quality of mercy but the masculine dimension of power as well. Ordinary people understood that evil in life could not be overcome solely with the help of the goddess's benevolence; a weak life wanting to grow and mature in safety needed the protection of a masculine god. This god was "Mount Taishan Rock Protector."

Mount Taishan is formed mainly of metamorphic rock and granites. It is very hard and for 2.5 billion years has undergone erosion by wind and rain, scorching sun and the scouring of ocean waves. Ages of weathering has shaped Mount Taishan's bare precipitous cliffs and huge hard rocks.

Its rocks have been held sacred and worshipped since antiquity.

Historical materials show that, for more than a thousand years, there have been examples of people erecting natural rocks, stone tablets or pillars engraved with the words "Mount Taishan Rock Protector" as a way of suppressing monsters and warding off evil. These would be positioned at important spots such as street corners, village entrances, bridges or at entrances to homes.

"Mount Taishan Rock Protector" embodies the most widely prevalent folk belief in China, covering everywhere but Tibet and Xinjiang. It influences the countries of Southeast and East Asia, and Chinese

Statue of Mount Taishan Rock Protector in front of the Temple of Mount Taishan

泰山石敢當

communities in Europe and America too. "Mount Taishan Rock Protector" has followed in the footsteps of Chinese people all over the world.

This folk belief originated with the ancient worship of mountains and sacred rocks. The remains of prehistoric sacrificial sites all have sacrificial altars built of stone. Even now, some ethnic minorities still maintain the custom of worshipping rocks, which they see as mountain gods. Every local mountain god is a guardian protecting the local area. Since ancient times,

The foundation stone of Overseas Chinese Plaza in Tai'an uses stone from Mount Taishan.

however, Mount Taishan has been thought of as the guardian of the whole

universe, giving rise to the saying "If Mount Taishan is at peace, the world is

Various sizes of Mount Taishan Rock Protector, for guarding the house and keeping the family safe

stable." In the Temple of Mount Taishan, the god is holding in his hands the distinguished jade tablet of guarding the universe. So if Mount Taishan has the power to guard the whole universe, it stands to reason that a small stone from Mount Taishan can protect the home!

With Mount Taishan guarding the country, the country is at peace;

With a Mount Taishan Rock Protector guarding the home, the family is safe.

Such is the significance of Mount Taishan to China and the Chinese.

This is why there are idioms like "as weighty as Mount Taishan," "as stable as Mount Taishan" and "as peaceful as Mount Taishan."

The name of Mount Taishan is a symbol, a promise of peace, a guarantee of stability and harmony. Under its silent protection, a Chinese person can feel its power and hear its blessing of safety wherever he goes.

Chapter VI

Mount Taishan and Buddhism

The Origin of Valley Mountain Temple

"Buddhism came from the west, and all famous mountains and beautiful landscapes turned into places of Buddhist ritual." This is the first sentence of the stele inscription *Record of Valley Mountain Temple* by Dang Huaiying, an academician and calligrapher of the Kin Dynasty (1115-1234).

In this inscription, Dang recorded the story of how long, long ago, a hunter went hunting on the Lotus Flower Peak of Mount Taishan and saw a stone statue of Buddha. By the end of the day, he had caught nothing. From then on, whenever he saw this Buddha he never had a successful hunt. Frustrated, the man collected a pile of dry wood and straw, ready to burn the statue next day. But when he came to light the fire, he was amazed to discover that the Buddha statue had moved to the top of a high cliff. That night, every old person and child at the foot of the mountain dreamed of a strange hermit monk living on Lotus Flower Peak. The following day, they went to the peak and found a stone Buddha Arhat between some rocks. They carried it down the mountain in a litter but when they got to the spot where Valley Mountain Temple now stands, the statue suddenly became too heavy to be carried. They looked around, saw that the site, surrounded by peaks, was a place of good geomantic omen, and thus built the Valley Mountain Temple on the spot.

The story indicates that during the Northern Wei Dynasty (386-534), there might have been Buddha niches in the cliff walls of some peaks of Mount Taishan. Could there possibly be Buddha niches on the summit itself?

Mahavira Hall of the Jade Spring Temple, situated on Guyu Mountain 20 kilometers north of the summit of Mount Taishan

Buddha Statue Discovered on the Summit

In 1985, beneath the little frequented Self-sacrifice Cliff on the summit of Mount Taishan, people unexpectedly came across a statue on the cliff face. In the 1.9-meter-high and 1.4-meter-wide niche is the carving of Bodhisattva Manjusri, Buddha of Wisdom, riding a lion. The moss and lichen-covered figure had an intrepid appearance and lean body. We know from the inscription beside the niche that it was carved in the Northern Song Dynasty (960-1127).

Bodhisattva of Wisdom under the Cliff of Self-sacrifice, discovered in 1985

This is the only Buddhist relic found so far on the top of Mount Taishan.

Whoever chose this site put a lot of thought into it. It is not visible from the top of Mount Taishan but it can be looked up to from below as visitors make their way up to the summit. The care that went into site selection shows the ingenuity of finding a hidden spot for Buddhism in the most conspicuous place on Mount Taishan as well as indirectly reflecting the situation of Buddhism on Mount Taishan.

Because Mount Taishan had already been a sacred mountain for Taoists to cultivate the Way before the advent of Buddhism, and because the mountain worship ceremonies affirmed the superior position of Taoism on the mountain, it would have been both foolish and futile for Buddhism, an alien religion, to try to take over from indigenous Taoism by occupying the mountain. The hidden site of the Buddha niche under the Self-sacrifice Cliff and the only half-finished carving confirm this.

Therefore, Buddhism tried to outflank Taoism on Mount Taishan in an indirect, long-term development strategy. If Taoism occupied the southern slope of the mountain, Buddhism would take over the northern part. If Taoism occupied the summit, Buddhism would take over the valley. If Taoism took places graced by heavenly wind, Buddhism would settle for gurgling creeks at the foot of the mountain. If Taoism demanded its disciples to climb high along the cliffs to emphasize the experience of hardships it required to achieve immortality, Buddhism would have its followers zigzagging in the woods, in steady and leisurely steps, to indicate Buddhism ensured them a smooth sailing.

Master Lang and Buddhism at Mount Taishan

It was in 351 that Buddhism was introduced to Mount Taishan from India. At the time China was divided into southern and northern parts; the Jin Dynasty court moved to the south, reigning only half of the country south of Huaibei. Northern China saw a succession of 16 small kingdoms where chaos ruled. A monk from Chang'an (today's Xi'an) living on Mount Kunrui at the southern foot of Mount Taishan built the first Buddhist temple. His monastic name was Lang, so people respectfully called this Buddhist temple the "Temple of Master Lang." The monk, a diligent teacher and strict about abstinence, made a big impact and the Temple of Master Lang developed fast, expanding to become the center of Buddhist culture in Shandong, a major temple with over ten courtyards, and a very long corridor linking up more than a thousand bays of rooms. The emperors of the Southern Yan, Northern Wei and Eastern Jin dynasties all donated money, presented treasures, and consulted about politics at the temple. Even when Emperor Taiwu (r. 424-452) of the Northern Wei Dynasty launched a large-scale attack on Buddhist temples, the Temple of

Where Master Lang preached Buddhism

Master Lang did not suffer destruction.

Yang Jian, Emperor Wen (r. 581-604) of the Sui Dynasty, was born in a Buddhist temple. His mother, from a poor family in Ji'nan, died at an early age. Having been raised by nuns, he had deep affection for Buddhism. In the second year of his reign, in memory of his mother he renamed the Temple of Master Lang as the Temple of Supernatural Power, the name chosen because of a dream in which Master Lang explained Buddhist scriptures to him and he became supernatural.

The Temple of Supernatural Power is famous in the history of Chinese Buddhism and was also the earliest Buddhist temple in Shandong. The temple lasted over 1,500 years but collapsed in the early 20th century, becoming a relic of history and leaving people with hazy memories and sense of nostalgia.

Some 20 kilometers northwest of the main peak of Mount Taishan, stands Square Mountain that resembles a city

Thousand Buddha Cliff on White Tiger Mountain, west of the Temple of Supernatural Power. Carved in the 7th century, it has 220 figures.

wall. The top of its main peak looks as if an axe has sliced through it. Because it also looks like the jade seal of ancient generals, it is also called Mount Jade Seal.

After Master Lang built the Temple of Supernatural Power, he often went to the Square Mountain to explain scriptures. To its south there was a tall, strange rock, perhaps ten meters high, which looked, from afar, like an old hunchbacked monk leaning on a walking stick and listening attentively to the scriptures. Once, when Master Lang was giving a lively lecture, some disciples saw this strange square rock nodding its head, and pointed at it, shouting: "Look, that rock understood. Even it was enlightened and is nodding!" Master Lang said: "Even the rocks here have souls!" At which he had the people dig the mountain and built a new Buddhist temple, and he named it Divine Rock Temple.

Divine Rock Temple and Its Group of Arhat Statues

Today's Divine Rock Temple is not the original, but was built in the early 7th century by the eminent monk Huichong. When Emperor Gaozong of Tang (r. 650-683) held the mountain worship ceremony at Taishan, it was here that he stayed. During the reign of Emperor Dezong (r. 780-805), his Prime Minister Li Jifu, ranked it highest among what he called "the Four Unique Places", the others being Guoqing (National Purity) Temple at Tiantai in Zhejiang, Yuquan (Jade Spring) Temple at Jiangling in Hubei and Qixia (Cloud Lingering) Temple at Nanjing. Clearly it

had a huge reputation. The custom of drinking tea in north China is said to have come from Divine Rock Temple!

The Thousand Buddha Palace, now the main building of the temple, has lavish decoration and upturning eaves.

The Thousand Buddha Palace enshrines three huge statues of Buddha. At the center is Vairocana Buddha, which was shaped in Hangzhou by the Song Dynasty monk Huicong and transported here. The Vairocana Buddha on the left and the Sakyamuni Buddha on the right were both made in the Ming Dynasty. All three figures are high and solemn; the molding and casting skills displayed are first class, but, from an artistic standpoint, they fall short of the 40 Arhats on the wall altar in the palace.

Thousand Buddha Palace at the Divine Rock Temple

Somewhat larger than life size, the Arhats were mostly created in the Song Dynasty and were renewed in 1124 by Miaokong, Abbot of the Divine Rock Temple, modeled on the original 500 Arhats.

In primitive Hinayana Buddhism, being an Arhat was the highest achievement. For Buddhists, Arhat is the highest degree, the end-result. Anyone who attains the highest achievement will never have to be reincarnated again and suffer the pain of transmigration of life and death. However, the Buddhist creed of saving all living creatures believes that if all the best Buddhists attained the status of Arhat, and extricated themselves by achieving Nirvana, who then would stay in the real world to spread Buddhism? Therefore, Mahayana Buddhism encourages Buddhists to be the Arhats who do not go to Nirvana but protect and preach Dharma. It is said when Sakyamuni was dying he appointed four monks to stay in the world to popularize the Law of Buddhism, stopping short of Nirvana. These four monks were the earliest four Arhats who lived in the world. Because the four were over-burdened with the task of spreading the Law, in some Buddhist scriptures, their numbers were increased to 16, and, later, two more were added, bringing the total to 18 Arhats.

Arhat worship started in the 10th century, during the Five Dynasties (907-960). In Buddhism, the 500 disciples of Sakyamuni are called "500 Arhats." From the Five Dynasties period, Buddhist temples in China began constructing many Arhat halls especially for the 500 Arhats. Because there were no rules for designing Arhat figures, artists could give their

An Arhat statue at the Thousand Buddha Palace

imagination full play, creating vivid, lively and characteristic Arhats, based on real monks and lay people — young and old, fat and thin, short and tall, ugly and handsome.

Abbot Miaokong thought the original Arhat figures were too crude, inappropriate for the famous Divine Rock Temple where so many Buddhist ceremonies were held. Therefore, he found a benefactor named Qi Gu to donate money and with these funds he had the figures of 500 Arhats made in Fujian, and then moved all the way to the Divine Rock Temple.

The Record of 500 Arhats of Divine Rock Temple described the 500 Arhats as having graceful manners, subtle expressions, huge bodies and odd images. Whether frowning or laughing, gazing or examining, lifting or lowering their heads, moving or still, they are all true to life and have different expressions. Their attitudes and personalities find expression in their eyes, brows, mouths and noses. Moreover, those parts not covered by clothes — necks, hands, muscles and bones — are finely detailed too. The carving is so exquisite that not only are the muscles and bones anatomically accurate, but also the blood vessels and veins can be seen clearly. The clothes and ornaments match very well the character's mentality and personality. The Northern Song Dynasty (960-1127) was a period of realism in Chinese modeling art, as demonstrated by this Arhat group at the Divine Rock Temple. The modern day scholar Liang Qichao accorded this group the highest praise, dubbing them the "first famous statues in the world."

The 500-Arhat project was huge and demanded a purpose-built Arhat Hall to accommodate them. Ordinary temples could not afford this, which gives an indication of the scale of the Divine Rock Temple in the Song Dynasty. But no one knows why, of the 500 Arhats, only 40 are left, some of which are obviously not the Song originals. For example, Master Ji was a monk in the Southern Song Dynasty (1127-1279). Humorous, fond of

defending people against injustice and helping the weak, Ji was very popular. But his figure could not possibly have existed among the 500 Arhats of the Northern Song Dynasty; it must have been made by later generations and installed there. In modern Arhat halls, people always put his statue in the hallway. In the Arhat Hall of the Azure Cloud Temple in Beijing, he crouches on the beam of the hall because he is late for the scripture lecture. The seats have all been taken. He has to stand at one side because he does not obey discipline.

The famous Ming Dynasty writer Wang Shizhen said: "It can't be called visiting Mount Taishan if you don't visit the Divine Rock Temple." The Divine Rock Temple, sitting in a surrounding of precipitous cliffs, gray rocks, flying springs, winding brooks, along with its palace halls and high pagodas, can certainly bring people to the tranquil Buddhist atmosphere in which one can meditate. If you ascend Mount Taishan without visiting the temple, you'll miss the most tranquil place on the mountain and the wonderful Buddhist culture of Mount Taishan. If we can see sunrise on the summit of Mount Taishan, cry long and loud with the wind at the South Gate to Heaven, and sit meditating for a while in the Pagoda Forest of the Divine Rock Temple, then the trip to Mount Taishan can come to a successful end.

The Pagodas of Mount Taishan

After Buddhism was introduced to China and fused with Chinese culture it started to generate a huge diversity of splendid pagodas.

On a hill southeast of the site of the Temple of Supernatural Power stands the solemn Four Door Pagoda, built in 611. It has a history of over 1,300 years and is China's oldest surviving stone pagoda.

The Four Door Pagoda is built totally with huge slabs of local "blue stone." Square in plan, and comprising one story, it has a semi-circular arched doorway on each side, hence the name Four Door Pagoda. Inside, in the middle of the pagoda stands a square stone column with a stone Buddha statue on every side of the column base. All have coiled hair buns, and sit cross-legged facing toward a doorway.

By its northeast corner stands a huge ancient pine tree that has nine roots extending out toward different directions; therefore, people call it the Nine Summit Pine Tree. The ancient pagoda and the ancient pine, both of them over a thousand years old, have witnessed too many calamities and disasters. Every visitor feels awe-struck standing here.

To the north of the Four Door Pagoda stands a brick and stone pagoda from the Tang Dynasty, called Dragon and Tiger Pagoda because of the carvings with which it is covered. Where the Four Door Pagoda is austere, this is lively and lavish. Each of its four faces has an arch opening, with flame patterns carved at either side and flanked by carvings of the four Heavenly Kings, holding a sword in one hand and a pagoda in the other and stamping on a demon. Above and at the four corners are delicate relief carvings of Arhats, flying Apsaras, deva-musicians, dragons and tigers. Inside the pagoda, at each corner there is a Buddha statue, characterized by lean faces and exquisite carving. This is an outstanding pagoda, one that combines elegant constructional design and superb carving techniques.

On the mid-level of the Divine Eagle Mountain, south of the site of the Temple of Supernatural Power, stands the unique Nine Steeple Pagoda, a relic of the Tang Dynasty. The shape and structure of the

The Four Door Pagoda

145

Pagoda Forest at the Divine Rock Temple

pagoda are very special. Basically it belongs in the pavilion-style category, but on top of it there stand nine small close-eave pagodas, hence the name of Nine Steeple. Its main body is a regular octagon, with each face concave, producing smooth and graceful lines. Its eaves resemble a blossoming lotus flower with more than ten layers of petals. This lotus flower in full bloom holds eight three-story pagodas, each of them about three meters in height, encircling a taller pagoda, over five meters in height, that stands, like a bud, at the center.

The Sending Clothes Pagoda is a square stone pagoda, similar to the Four Door Pagoda in shape and structure. It was first built in the Tang Dynasty. In the past, the monks would give dirty and worn out clothes to the nuns at this very spot, who would return them clean and mended, hence the name of the pagoda.

On the site of the Temple of Supernatural Power, there are still more than 40 stone or brick tomb pagodas of temple abbots during the Kin, Yuan, Ming and Qing dynasties. They are called the Forest of Buddhist Masters. There is a pair of stone statues in the forest, which, unless you examine their inscriptions, you would not take to be pagodas. There is no Buddhist imagery: no steeples, Buddhist pictures or figures, even the lotus petal-shaped bases that tomb pagodas or Buddhist structures usually use are absent. Indeed, the pagoda body is carved with peonies, chrysanthemums and sunflowers, and the three-level steeple has the shape of a Han Dynasty style gable and hip roof. But it is, in fact, the tomb

Dragon and Tiger Pagoda

The Nine Steeple Pagoda

The Pratyeka Pagoda

pagoda of Master Wuwei, an abbot of the Temple of Supernatural Power during the Ming Dynasty. In the architectural history of Chinese pagodas, the designer of this pagoda was really a great reformer; his unconventional spirit, brave innovation and his striving for national style architecture still provide a good example for modern people.

The Pagoda Forest of the Divine Rock Temple boasts 167 tomb pagodas, erected between the Tang and Qing dynasties in memory of the temple's abbots and eminent monks. Among all China's pagoda forests, this one is very rare because of the large number, long history, rich types and elegant designs of the tomb pagodas concentrated here. The earliest one is the Abbot Huicong Pagoda, erected during the Tianbao (742-756) reign period of the Tang Dynasty.

Beside the tomb pagoda of Xian, the 39th Abbot of the Divine Rock Temple, stands the Stele of the Moral Conduct of Abbot Xian written by a Japanese eminent monk Shaoyuan who came to China in 1327 and stayed studying in many famous monasteries for 21 years. He was a first-rank monk at the Shaolin Temple on Songshan Mountain and had a deep friendship with Abbot Xian who was the 15th abbot there.

To the right of the Thousand Buddha Palace is the Pratyeka Pagoda that was built in the Tianbao (742-756) reign period and rebuilt in the mid-11th century. Pratyeka is also a name of Buddha, meaning "self-enlightenment," namely, to become Buddha through learning by oneself. When the Pratyeka Buddha was born, Sakyamuni had died, and there was no one who could teach him, so he had to learn by himself. The Pratyeka Pagoda is 54 meters tall, built of brick and stone. The bottom of the pagoda is a stone base. On four sides of the base are carvings of hell and various cruel punishments, a very rare phenomenon in Buddhist pagoda ornamentation. Perhaps this has something to do with the Mount Taishan hell legends. The iron steeple on top of the pagoda towers into the clouds. From the top of the steeple eight iron chains extend to the eight corners of the pagoda top. Eight iron warrior attendants stand on the drooping ridges.

Monastery of Omnipresent Light, Buddhism and Confucianism

The ancient Puzhao Temple or Monastery of Omnipresent Light was built over 1,500 years ago. Situated on the northern side of the mountain ring road in Tai'an, the temple stands in front of Linghan Peak, surrounded by mountains and hidden among green pines. A clear stream flows to one side of it. The temple buildings, a complete Buddhist monastery complex, stretch across the mountainside.

It comprises four courts, set along the axis between the two main gates, the Grand Hall of the Buddha and the Pine Tower. Living quarters, monastic meditation rooms and gardens are arranged east and west of the courts.

But the essence of this monastery is neither its architecture nor even its Buddha. What really draw people to it are two ancient pine trees.

One of them, known as the famous Six Dynasty Pines, is huge and strong, with branches stretching out in all directions, like huge imperial carriage canopies. The exuberant branch network and foliage are like a green

Moonlight Sifting Pavilion in the Monastery of Omnipresent Light

150

net cast across the sky. Sunlight and moonlight filter through this green net, leaving dappled shadows on the ground. Close by stands the Moonlight Sifting Pavilion, named from a line in an old poem: "Tall pines sift the moonlight." In the pavilion there is a square stone table that emits clear musical notes when hit on the four corners and the center.

The Grand Master Pine was first named "Junior Apprentice Pine" and planted by Monk Lixiu when he came to the monastery. Lixiu personified the tree, affectionately referred to it as his fellow junior apprentice and wrote a very touching poem: "The monk

The main entrance to the Monastery of Omnipresent Light

The Korean eminent monk Mankong came across the sea to Mount Taishan and rebuilt the Monastery of Omnipresent Light. After his death, his disciples set up a stone tablet inscribed with his stories.

The Grand Master Pine

planted the pine, the pine offers shades to the monk; you and I live together like brothers. The pine is the monk, and the monk is the pine; we both follow Buddhism, so we are brothers." The seedling later grew up into a huge, upright and very handsome tree which people called the Grand Master Pine.

East of the monastery lie the remains of a stone building. This was the stone hall where Abbot Yuanyu of the Monastery of Omnipresent Light drank and sang and created poems with his friends.

A closer look at Yuanyu may give us an understanding of Buddhism's later evolution on Mount Taishan. What the Buddhist disciple Yuanyu did, in this land which was the birthplace of Confucianism, was to pull Buddhism toward Confucianism. When expounding on Buddhism he would always talk about the Confucian concepts of "three cardinal guides and five constant virtues" He believed loyalty and filialty to be benevolence advocated by Buddhism and also human nature. He emphasized reality rather than the division between monastic and secular life. What he was trying to do was to turn Buddhism away from monasticism and the renunciation of human society into a lay religion strongly imbued with

Confucianism. For the stele inscription recording the rebuilding of the Monastery of Omnipresent Light, he wrote: "The benevolence and virtue of Confucianism are the compassion of Sakyamuni." Yuanyu burned three josses of incense every morning on rising. The first joss was — not to worship Buddha, but always to pray for long life for the emperor! In the Moonlight Sifting Pavilion, there is a couplet that goes: "To introduce a spring, to plant bamboos and open up three pathways; to bring Buddhism closer to Confucianism and approach the five saints." This very clearly shows Yuanyu's intention of bring Buddhism closer to Confucianism. His famous words about Mount Taishan are an expression of Confucian social ideals: "May people all over the world live in peace, then Mount Taishan will live in peace; May people all over the world live in safety, then Mount Taishan will be safe. If there is one person who can't live in safety, then Mount Taishan is not safe; if there is one person who can't live in peace, then Mount Taishan is not peaceful."

The Chinese people, from emperors to common folk, endowed Mount Taishan with the sacred duty of keeping the country stable and people safe. Any religion attached to Mount Taishan must implement this duty if it wanted to establish itself.

Buddhist temples on Mount Taishan are usually situated on the northern slope, or at the northeast foot or northwest foot, so as to avoid confrontation with Taoism. The only

Stone carved with the image of Yuanyu in the Monastery of Omnipresent Light

exceptions are the Monastery of Omnipresent Light and the Bamboo Forest Temple, both located on the southern slope. The Bamboo Forest Temple disappeared in the Qing Dynasty but was rebuilt in 2,000 in accordance with Tang architectural style. Examining the sites of these two Buddhist temples, even though they are on the southern slope of Mount Taishan, they are tucked away, hidden in the mountain and remote from the main path. Thus, although Buddhism has been present on Mount Taishan throughout history and established a foothold on there, as an alien culture, it could never dominate Mount Taishan or become its mainstream culture. Buddhism at Mount Taishan has always been something of an appendage.

Buddhism Assimilated by Mount Taishan

In order to get a position on the main path of Mount Taishan, Buddhism adopted an infiltration approach, involving several ploys. First it disguised the Bodhisattva Guanyin or Goddess of Mercy, worshipped the most by common Chinese people, as a god with Taoist characteristics, and then placed it in the Taoist temples along the main path. The tactic was extremely successful: Guanyin was able to share worshippers' incense with the Taoist goddesses Big Dipper Mother and Bixia Yuanjun (Supreme Monarch of Azure Cloud).

Second, it occupied parts of the Taoist temples. From the 14th century on, Buddhist nuns started to become the owners of the palaces of Big Dipper Mother in Taoist temples. Here the new owners not only built halls for the White-robe Goddess

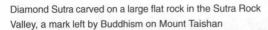

Diamond Sutra carved on a large flat rock in the Sutra Rock Valley, a mark left by Buddhism on Mount Taishan

Sutra Rock Valley

of Mercy, but also changed the orientation of the main gate and reversed the positions of the White-robe Hall and the Hall of Big Dipper Mother, making the Buddhist former side hall into the main hall, and demoting the Taoist main hall to side hall status. However, from the stele inscription Record of Building the White-robe Hall in the Palace of Big Dipper Mother, we can see that to win over worshippers, Buddhism had to lean toward folk religion, Taoism, and associate closely with the common Chinese people's needs.

Today, both in the Red Gate Palace and the Palace of Big Dipper Mother, we can see Buddhist and Taoist goddesses in an intriguing example of two religions side by side in the same temple.

In the Tang Dynasty, Buddhist monks were very confident as revealed by

Inscription, dating from 570, of the Prajnaparamita Sutra, on Reflecting Buddha Cliff at the top of Liangfu Mountain, southeast of Mount Culai. The inscription, in official script, is on three levels, comprising 131 characters about 40 centimeters high and is a key cultural relic under province-level protection.

Bamboo Forest Temple, rebuilt in 2,000 reproducing Tang Dynasty (618-907) architectural style. The date of the first temple is unknown; it has been destroyed and rebuilt many times since the Tang.

the inscription on the stone tablet in the Temple of Sacred Treasures, engraved in 736, which reads: "Sakyamuni saw the moral depravity of China in the East, which Confucianism and Taoism were powerless to stop. Therefore, Sakyamuni undertook this trip of benevolence and brought Buddhist scriptures on his white horse. He came to China to deliver the people in the East from their misery."

It is very clear that Buddhism did harbor strong confidence of converting Mount Taishan to its faith.

Buddhist scriptures were carved on mountains like Yishan Mountain, Liangfu Mountain and Jingshi Valley. The sites were so deliberately chosen that clearly Buddhism was pointing to the direction of the base camp of Confucianism, Taoism's caves of immortals, and the sacred mountain where national Taoism had been established.

To carve Buddha statues on the summit of Mount Taishan revealed

From the east side of Sun Facing Cave looking north, the mountain range appears like a huge male Buddha lying on Flying Dragon Rock and a huge female Buddha lying on Hovering Phoenix Peak, both facing the blue sky. Buddhism and mountains blending — one of the wonders of Mount Taishan

Below the South Gate to Heaven, a huge rock protrudes from the western cliff. In profile it looks like the head of a Buddha emerging from the mountainside, with a high nose and cheekbones and a protruding forehead. It seems to be gently smiling.

Shenxiao Mountain on the eastern side of the summit of Mount Taishan, looking very much like a Bodhisattva standing against the mountain and overlooking the world

Buddhism's intention of attacking the main peak of the mountain.

Buddhism planted the Monastery of Omnipresent Light and Bamboo Forest Temple on the southern slope of Mount Taishan. Perhaps it had hoped to use the two temples as springboards to move deeper into the Taoist home on the mountain.

To infiltrate the Taoist temples and nunneries on the main pathway to the mountain summit indicated that Buddhism was prepared to fight a protracted war with Taoism.

When Taoism was content with be-

ing the dominant religion on Mount Taishan and happy to stay as the official belief, Buddhism actively went into the villages to have one after another temple erected where people lived, completing an encirclement of the main peak of Mount Taishan.

Ultimately the more Buddhism tried to encroach on Mount Taishan, however, the more it lost. In the end, it was Mount Taishan that assimilated Buddhism.

This, then, is Mount Taishan. Its openness to both domestic and foreign religions is as great as its firm stand in maintaining its own faith.

Chapter VII

Mount Taishan and Confucianism

Confucius ascends Mount Taishan

It was a fine day with clear autumn skies when the sage Confucius came to Mount Taishan with his best student Yan Yuan — two men of great thoughts drawn for some reason to the summit of Mount Taishan in the troubled times of the Spring and Autumn Period (722-481 BC). From the Wangwu Peak east of the Heavenly Street, and gazing south as far as he could see, Confucius made out the capital of the State of Wu hundreds of miles away, today's Suzhou, where he saw a white horse tethered outside the city gate. Confucius beckoned Yan Yuan, and, point-

ing to the southeast, asked him: "Have you seen the city gate of the State of Wu?" "I saw a white tether." Immediately Confucius put his hand over Yan's eyes to stop him seeing further. When they got to the foot of the mountain, all Yan's teeth had fallen and his hair had gone white.

That same day, Confucius climbed the Zhanlu Terrace (Terrace for Viewing Lu) to overlook his homeland, and then climbed the Qinguan Peak to look toward the Central Plains and the State of Qin in Central Shaanxi. Gazing across the vast blue yonder, his heart was grasped with sorrow; this was a world where rites and music had been destroyed!

So, one of the grandest sights in the

Zhanlu Terrace (Terrace for Viewing Lu)

162

Spot where Confucius stood on the mountain

history of human thought appeared on the peak of Mount Taishan: a tall old man with a long beard stood alone on the summit of Mount Taishan, gazing in silence at the war-torn land. He was so high minded and yet so solitary. In the then world, there was no one who understood his thoughts and aspirations. Given his wisdom, character and ideals, this great man of the Spring and Autumn Period had reason enough for ascending Mount Taishan and finding the smallness of the empire.

The philosophical significance of Confucius ascending Mount Taishan and realizing the smallness of the empire was a much more profound and far-reaching event than imperial mountain worship ceremonies. The lonely ascent and silent gazing out, the coming together of the sage and the holy mountain was a defining moment in Chinese thought and culture; nothing can compare with it. It is a high point looking down over the morality and justice of China.

There is a rock in the west of the Bixia Temple called the "Confucius Cliff." Despite the mosses and water streaks on the rock face, the inscription, dating from the the Jiaqing reign (1796-1820) of the Qing Dynasty, is still clear: "Confucius is a sage like Mount Taishan, and Mount Taishan is a saint mountain like Confucius. If you can maintain your sangfroid when meeting with big things, you have a Mount Taishan in your heart...."

Confucius praises mountains

Confucius was also named Kong Qiu and styled Zhong Ni. The name was a reference to Mount Ni Qiu, which stands southeast of Qufu City. His 66-year-old father and 20-year-old mother very much wanted a child, so they went to Mount Ni Qiu to pray to the mountain god. On the way back they stopped to rest in a cave, where, much to their surprise, the mother suddenly gave birth to Confucius. The old father and young mother were both overjoyed and named their child after this mountain which they believed had brought them the child.

Born from the prayer to a mountain and named after the mountain, the legend of the birth of Confucius is tinged with a kind of primitive mountain worship. Perhaps it was precisely because of this mysterious connection that Confucius forged an indissoluble bond with mountains that lasted a lifetime, and was so sensitive about the image and spirit of mountains. This philosopher with the sensitivity of a poet was always climbing mountains and wandering by rivers in search of inspiration and refining his sentiments. He said: "The be-nevolent take delight in mountains and the wise in water."

His cleverest student Zi Gong once asked him: "Why do the benevolent take delight in mountains?" The sage replied: "You see the mountains: their grandeur brings them the respect and admiration of people. All kinds of plants grow on them. Birds and animals live and multiply in their forests. Mountains produce many mountain treasures and contain all kinds of mines. And they are also good places for great scholars and eminent people to retreat from the world. The greatness of mountains is that they never tire of supporting all lives and never begrudge providing for the needs of people around. The winds and clouds that emerge from the mountains become the breath of life that fills the world. If there were no mountains to provide people with their needs, how could countries come into being? This is why the benevolent take delight in mountains."

The Song Dynasty thinker Zhu Xi thought that the reason the benevolent like mountains is because they can see features similar to their own characters in the image of mountains. The benevolent all focus on justice and truth, strong-willed, never changing their stands, never ceasing in their search for truth. Their personality is as lofty as the mountains, their moral character as grand, their sentiments as exalted and their will as strong.

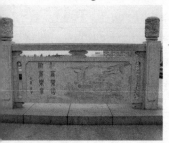

"The benevolent take delight in mountains and the wise in water." Words of Confucius inscribed on stone panel at Heaven and Earth Square

164

Confucius' respect for Mount Taishan

In 484 BC, the 68-year-old Confucius returned to the State of Lu, bringing an end to 14 years of homelessness and drifting between different states. He bent himself to the task of editing literature and teaching students. He cut some parts of the *Book of Songs* and *Collection of Classics,* finalized the *Book of Rites* and the *Classic of Music,* revised *The Spring and Autumn Annals,* and continued training students in the management of state affairs.

The *Book of Songs* revised and finalized by Confucius is China's first collection of poetry. The last poem in the volume entitled *Lu Song (Sacrificial Songs of the State of Lu)* in the collection is an epic relating the history of the State of Lu. In this poem, which was a paean of praise to their ancestors sung by the descendants of the Duke of Zhou during sacrifice ceremonies, are the lines: "The lofty Mount Taishan is the pride of our State of Lu; its grand form is the sign of the northern border of Lu. The Lu land is so great that all lands from the Tortoise Peak and Meng Peak at the foot of Mount Taishan to the end of the earth bordering the East Sea all belong to the State of Lu. Even the aboriginals living beside the sea admire and attach themselves to the State of Lu. All of these result from the management

by rites of dukes of the State of Lu."

This *Lu Song* dating from the Western Zhou Dynasty (11th century-771 BC) gives us an insight into the status of Mount Taishan in the minds of the people of Lu. By means of metaphor, the poem describes Mount Taishan as the symbol of rule by virtue and rite, admired by all eastern states. It proudly lauds the merits of the State of Lu spreading its culture eastward. We don't know whether Confucius interpolated some of his own opinions in the process of revising and finalizing the work, but what we can be certain of is that the poem clearly expresses Confucius' approval of the Zhou ritual, and his admiration of Mount Taishan. To Confucius, Mount Taishan was not just the home mountain of his native Lu, but also the symbol of the Zhou ritual, complete in every respect; it was a sacred mountain of spirit and culture.

Ji Sun, a powerful senior official in the State of Lu, suddenly decided to offer sacrifices to the God of Mount Taishan. Confucius was shocked to the core, deeming that only kings were qualified to perform this rite. How dare the subordinate of a duke presume to do so? He asked his student Ran You, who was also the chamberlain of the Ji Sun family, to talk his master out it, but Ran You said he was helpless and Ji Sun did go to Mount Taishan. Confucius switched his anger to

Confucius' student Lin Fang (from *Xintai Culture*)

The tomb of Zi Gong was in front of the tomb of Confucius, where Zi Gong had built a hut to observe mourning for his teacher.

Mount Taishan: "Alas! Is it true that the God of Mount Taishan knows less about rites than my student Lin Fang?"

Lin Fang was from Mount Taishan. He once asked Confucius about the basis of the rite. His birthplace was since named after him and is now known as Fangcheng (Fang Town). Confucius did Mount Taishan an injustice, but thanks to Confucius' praise, Lin Fang's name has lived on to become a shining example of people from Mount Taishan and their knowledge of rites. The Tang Emperor Xuanzong granted him the title of Count of Qinghe, and the Song Emperor Zhenzong made him Marquis of Changshan. Later generations built the Temple of the Sage of Lin Fang for people to admire and respect him.

Lin Fang had made a thorough study of rites, so Confucius regarded him highly. Once, he and Lin came to Shiyazi, not far from Lin's homeplace. Standing here, looking south, seeing the unceasing flow of the torrential river water, Confucius could not help sighing with emotion: "The passage of time is just like this river, flowing away day and night, never stopping. Once gone, it never returns." Echoing down the centuries these words have become a well-known adage.

The Confucius Temple on the Summit

Up the stone steps by the Memorial Arch of the Sacred Place for Viewing the State of Wu, is the Temple of Confucius on the Summit of Mount Taishan. This is the only example of a mountain temple to Confucius in China: Confucius temples were usually set in cities, and served not only as places to offer sacrifices to Confucius, but also as schools for officials of counties and prefectures. The Temple of Confucius on the summit of Mount Taishan is the only one on a high mountain, which fact indicates the high status of Mount Taishan in the eyes of Confucian disciples. This Temple of Confucius was built by a court minister Zhu Heng during the Jiangjing reign period of the Ming Dynasty (1522-1566) and repaired by Zha Zhilong during the Wanli reign (1573-1620). In the early 20th century, when China was being fought over by warlords, the temple was dismantled by the Shanxi army guarding Mount Taishan for building works. It has now been restored.

The temple once had stone statues, and people would come to offer sacrifices not just to Confucius, but also to the statues of his disciples Yan Yuan, Zeng Shen, Zi Si and Mencius.

Temple of Confucius on the summit of Mount Taishan

Painting of Confucius

The memorial arch, built by later generations to mark the spot where, according to legend, Confucius and Yan Yuan looked out at the distant State of Wu

168

Confucius' Disciples from Mount Taishan

Confucius established his own school and began teaching followers at the age of 30, and did not stop until his death at 73. Because of his encyclopedic knowledge and great virtue, his disciples grew in number, coming not only from the states of Qi and Lu, but from all other major states — Chu, Jin, Qin, Chen and Wu. It is said that he had more than 3,000 students over his lifetime; among these were 72 outstanding students, many of them from poor families, who were good at skills previously reserved for the nobility — namely "rites, music, archery, driving horses, writing and mathematics."

Yan Yuan was the student Confucius liked best, because despite living in a mean alley on simple fare, he was nevertheless cheerful and uncomplainingly insisted on studying hard so as to temper his moral character and virtues.

Zeng Shen was another famous student of Confucius from Mount Taishan. Renowned for his filial piety and self-cultivation, throughout his life Zeng was hypercritical about his daily conduct, intolerant of any faults and weaknesses in his nature, conducting self-examination three times a day. He is said to have written the *Classic of Filial Piety*. He was also one of Confucius' youngest students. In his early years he farmed at the foot of Mount Taishan, and wrote the famous poem *The Recitation of Father Liang*.

You Ruo, a native of Youjia Village at the foot of Mount Taishan, was another of Confucius' youngest student. It was You who made the famous argument: "If the people are satisfied, how can the ruler not be satisfied? How can the ruler be satisfied if his people are not?" and "In conducting the rites, seeking harmony is the most valuable principle." You looked like Confucius, so after their teacher's death, people treated him as if he were Confucius.

Ran Geng, from Ranjia Village southwest of Feicheng, was one of Confucius' oldest students, only seven years younger than the master himself. He was as well-known for his virtues as for his caution in deed or word. Unfortunately, he contracted leprosy, but Confucius made a special journey to see him before he died, taking his hand from outside the window and calling to him sorrowfully. The village has a Master Ran Temple for the clan to offer sacrifices to him. As a demonstration of special favor to the descendants of Ran, the Qing Court once set official positions, specially for the Ran clan.

Confucius was the first thinker in Chinese cultural history to discover the value of man. His concept of "benevolent governance" emphasized the democratic nature and humanitarianism within the primitive clan system. While his economic and political ideas supported the hierarchical system of feudal society, he was against excess, barbarity and naked oppression and exploitation. More importantly, as the first great educator in Chinese history, his concept of "in teaching, treat everyone the same" broke down class barriers in training talent and inculcating knowledge; his setting up his own school was a milestone in cultural and educational history, making "knowledge and skills a common resource." He particularly focused his students' spiritual growth. He found the dignity and honor of human nature. He believed that everybody has a responsibility to history and that in order to be able to fulfill this duty, people should, through constant study and education, perfect their character, search for knowledge, study hard, train their will power, painstakingly cultivate themselves, finally achieving "benevolence." Anyone reaching this state could be called a gentleman. "If a man can be entrusted with a young ruler and the destiny of a state, and if in a moment of crisis, he does not waver — can he be counted as a gentleman? He is indeed a gentleman."

The Almond Altar in the Temple of Confucius at Qufu, where Confucius gave classes.

Confucius' Encounters on Mount Taishan

Mount Taishan has high peaks and deep valleys, so tigers were common on the mountain. The Qing Emperor Qianlong once shot dead a tiger there. Once when Confucius was leading his students to pass by Mount Taishan, he saw a woman crying by a graveside and sent Zi Lu to ask why. "Some evil thing must have happened to you to make you so miserable!" said Zi Lu to the woman. She replied: "Yes. Before this, my husband's father was eaten by a tiger and later he himself was eaten. And now a tiger has eaten my son, too!" Puzzled, Zi Lu asked her: "Well, why haven't you left this place?" "There're no exorbitant taxes and levies here," the woman answered. When Zi Lu reported back to Confucius, the master said to the other students: "Remember this: tyranny that exploits the blood and sweat of the people is more vicious than a tiger."

At the foot of Mount Taishan, Confucius met a strange old man named Zhong Qiqi, who might be a hermit on the mountain. Wearing deerskin, sporting a long silver beard, sitting on a rock, playing a *qin* harp without any decoration or carvings. Confucius bowed to him and asked: "Sir, why are you so happy?" The man replied "Man is the most precious of all living creatures, and thinking of this makes me happy. In terms of human beings, man is more honorable than woman, so the fact that I was born a man makes me very happy. People have different life spans, some dying young, while I am now 95 years old. How could I not be happy at such good health? With these three blessings, what have I got to be sad about?" He continued: "Nobody likes poverty, but being poor is actually what scholars should be; everybody fears death, but death is the end-result of life. Why should people worry?" Confucius praised these words, thinking that Zhong Qiqi was a man good at consolation and self-satisfaction. However, Zhong Qiqi's words did not stop Confucius wondering from state to state. Clever hermits poked fun at him as a "homeless dog," and advised him to give up his unrealizable social ideals. Confucius was not swayed, but continued traveling between states on an oxcart, leading his followers, in the spirit of "Knowing the hopelessness of something but doing it anyway." The sound of his oxcart wheels rolling across the Spring and Autumn landscape, the songs and poetry sung by the master and students along the road, were to re-echo in the skies of history for ever.

Mencius, like Mount Taishan in Character

Second only to Confucius was Mencius, also known as Meng Ke and referred to as "the lesser sage."

Confucius was born as the result of his parents' prayers to the Mount Ni Qiu, while the birth of Mencius was directly related with Mount Taishan. It was said that Mencius' mother had a dream that she was embracing Mount Taishan, and that when she awoke, she was pregnant. Later she gave birth to Mencius.

In Confucius' opinion, the ideal character was that of the gentleman (*junzi*) in whom simplicity and refinement were well-balanced. The rite situation at the time of Mencius (a.372-289 BC) was even worse than when Confucius was alive. So in his mind the ideal character was the true man (*dazhangfu*) with moral force. That is:

For males, the guiding principle should be benevolence. His performance should conform to the rites and his behavior should be righteous and just. When he is in power, he should follow the right course together with the people; when he is not in power, he should stick to his own principles. Wealth and power cannot corrupt him, poverty cannot sway his principles and threats cannot make him bend. Only such a person can be called a true man.

When heaven intends to bestow a great mission on a person, it makes him suffer in mind and body. It makes him endure starvation, and subjects him to poverty, difficulties and all kinds of tests so as to harden his will power, toughen his nature and increase his capabilities.

Life is what I treasure and righteousness is also what I treasure. If I cannot have both, I prefer righteousness to life.

These stirring words, which have remained very popular for 2,000 years, were the ideal character that Mencius set for Chinese with high aspirations. It focuses on the gentleman's moral self-discipline, emphasizing individual values, moral responsibility and historical duty. It was precisely due to Mencius' elevating moral character as the main principle, that the nature of the gentleman was established in Chinese culture. As a great creation in the history of Chinese thought, it has had an immeasurable influence in shaping the character of the Chinese people. Because the character of the true man put forward by Mencius was great and strong, similar to the image of Mount Taishan, Confucian followers of later ages praised Mencius as "having the character of rocky Mount Taishan."

Mencius is said to have been born in the hamlet called Fucun, in the west of the Mengmu (Mencius' Mother) Forest. In the village, is the former residence of Mencius, a three-room house surrounded by trees, by a creek with a bridge across it. Behind the house is an ancient well called Mengmu (Mencius' Mother) Well. As a child Mencius was certainly very naughty. By his home, there was a graveyard where funeral ceremonies were always held. The silly little Mencius was always playing games to do with the dead. His mother thought this was harmful so they moved to Miaohuying Village.

Miaohuying, located in the southwest of Zouxian County, was said to be a busy market then. Little Mencius began to learn how to boast and show off from the market traders, so his mother moved the family again to a new home beside the official school.

The site of the official school was beside the Yinli Aqueduct at Nanguan, in Zouxian County. After Mencius' family moved here, he began to study with the scholars of the school and rehearse the rites of "making bows with hands folded in front, and stepping forward and back." His mother was very happy about this, and they finally settled down here.

But settling down beside the school did not tame Mencius' mischievous spirit. Once when he played truant and went back home, his mother was so distressed she cut through the cloth she was in the process of weaving and said to the boy: "If you don't study hard, giving up your studies halfway, just like this cut cloth, what use will you be when you are grown?" Hearing these

Cliff inscription on the summit of Mount Taishan, the characters "Yan Yan" (rocky rock) expressing the respect and honor of people of all ages to Mount Taishan and to Mencius' Mount Taishan-like spirit

words, the young Mencius was ashamed of his former conduct. He began studying hard, and finally became a great Confucian scholar. People respected him and considered him as the second generation, direct inheritor of Confucian orthodoxy. For his shining contribution to Chinese culture, he was seen as "the lesser sage," second only to Confucius himself.

The gentleness and scholarly nature of Confucius, and the will power and noble spirit of Mencius permeated the rocky Mount Taishan with the character of Confucianism. Like Mount Taishan itself, these two great men from the ancient states of Zouxian and Lu will live for ever.

The Avid Students of Lu

The Song Dynasty gave birth to a generation of famous Confucian scholars and a rejuvenation of Confucian ideas. Scholars from Mount Taishan made very important contributions to this flowering of Confucianism. Sun Fu, Shi Jie and Hu Yuan established the Mount Taishan Academy and taught students there. They deemed it their own responsibility to inherit and spread Confucian orthodoxy.

Sun Fu (992-1057), dubbed "Master Mount Taishan," was so poor that, even though over 40, he could not afford to take a wife, but he still worked very hard at writing books. Although of humble social status, he concerned himself with the affairs of the country. His in-depth abstract treatise on centralism for the not long established Northern Song Dynasty was highly regarded by politicians of the time, including Fan Zhongyan. The Mount Taishan Academy was the place where he taught the meaning and significance of the Confucian classics.

Shi Jie (1005-1045) enjoyed higher social and official status than Sun, but he enthusiastically arranged his classes at the academy and showed him all the respect owed to a teacher. Whenever Sun Fu delivered lessons or had guests, Shi Jie would stand aside to serve. In whatever he said and did, Shi Jie set a good example of honoring the teacher and respecting the truth.

Hu Yuan (993-1059) who came from Taizhou in Jiangsu was such a diligent student he forgot to eat or sleep when studying in the Mount Taishan Academy. Every time he received letters from home, if he saw the words at the beginning "all OK," he would read no further but tear it up and throw it in the nearby stream, so as to save time for

Mount Taishan Academy behind the Temple of Omnipresent Light

study. Throwing himself into study, he did not go home for ten years. He was the first scholar in China to expound clearly on freedom of thought and science. His view was that that the thinking of a politician in authority should not exceed what is proper, because of his political responsibilities to society; for a scholar, on the other hand, "nothing should be unthinkable, nothing unsayable." Being without social political responsibilities, there should be no no-go areas for his thinking, he should be true to his thought and develop his own theories.

Later, Sun Fu, Shi Jie and Hu Yuan all went to teach at the Imperial College of the Song Dynasty, attracting students from all over China. They became famous scholars and educators of the early Song and pioneers of the *lixue* (Neo-Confucianism) of the Song and Ming dynasties. The famous Song Neo-Confucians Cheng Yi and Zhu Xi were always referring to these three men. As a mark of their respect, people called them "the three masters of the early Song." The place they taught had previously been a Taoist temple, and after their death, the locals built the "Temple of Three Masters" on the site. In the Daoguang reign period (1821-1850), of the Qing Dynasty, its name was changed to "Temple of Five Masters," following the addition of statues of two more Mount Taishan Confucian masters, namely the Ming Dynasty censor Song Tao and Zhao Guolin, an imperial academician dur-

Stone inscription of the Temple of Five Masters at the Temple of Omnipresent Light

ing the Kangxi reign period of the Qing Dynasty.

The Mount Taishan Academy established by the three masters was highly praised by their contemporary and man of letters Ouyang Xiu. He said that the school began the tradition that was able to "make everyone in Lu an avid student." The reason why later statues could be added to receive respects and honor at the Temple of Five Masters was because they established the Qingyan Academy in Tai'an, inheritors of the teaching tradition of the three masters.

In the early 1930s, General Feng Yuxiang retired from the army to Mount Taishan. He read *The Spring and Autumn Annals* in the Temple of Five Masters. Inspired by the educational spirit of the five masters, he established 15 schools to educate people, and transform their old ideas. Over 800 children from poor family background were given the chance of schooling, as the schools demanded no tuition fees and even provided with food and clothing.

Millennia-old Moral Lessons

In 1931, Zhao Xinru, an eminent scholar of Tai'an, wrote a couplet in the Temple of Five Masters: "The 72 emperors who held mountain worship ceremonies on Mount Taishan, which dynasties they belonged to? Where now lie the territories of each dynasty, around these green mountains and rivers? In 500 years famous scholars, one after the other, have been penning their own moral essays that often lodge in the ancestral temple on Mount Taishan." Indeed, kings and emperors were the passing travelers of history. No imperial dynasty could have that life as everlasting as Mount Taishan for which they prayed; nor could any emperor carve such a perennially great image deep into the Chinese soul. No matter how hard you scour Chinese history, there is only one person and theory as closely bound up as Mount Taishan with the spiritual life of the Chinese people. That person is Confucius.

At the entrance of the Red Gate Maitreya Temple is a rock, inscribed with words "Rocky Mount Taishan," taken

The Temple of Confucius at Qufu, hometown of Confucius, where the Confucian clan offer sacrifices to their ancestor.

from the the *Book of Songs*. This is said to be the very rock where Confucius sighed: "The people of Lu look with reverence to Rocky Mount Taishan." Of course, this is a dubious modern conclusion with no historical evidence to prove it. What is of real interest is a nearby stone board about two meters long, on which is carved a *weiqi* (go) board and *weiqi* pieces. The black player's poem reads: "We take stones as our pieces, the ground as our chessboard; this great game is nearing its end." There is a poem from the white player too: "Where are the *qin*-playing Taoist and the poet monk? Only this green mountain is still rocky." It is a Ming Dynasty style chessboard. It is said that a Buddhist monk from the Temple of Omnipresent Light and a Taoist priest from the Mother of Big Dipper Temple played chess, but since neither could defeat the other, they had to finish the game as a stalemate.

The chess match symbolizes the struggle between Taoism and Buddhism on Mount Taishan, a struggle that ended in stalemate. The western part of the Red Gate Palace is the Taoist "Yuanjun Temple," and the eastern part the Buddhist "Maitreya Temple," which illustrates the fact of the merging of Buddhism and Taoism. However, the real winner lies hiding behind. On the chess game, the black and white pieces were stalemated, but they all depended on the "rock" that was the

board. From this, it is easy to discover the real winner on Mount Taishan. The Confucian belief in "the rocky Mount Taishan to which the Lu people look with reverence" was the spiritual pillar uniting Taoism, Buddhism and Confucianism. Is not the historical summation: "Where are the *qin*-playing Taoist and the poet monk? Only this green mountain is still rocky?" confirmed by the inscriptions carved on temple walls such as "as stable as Mount Taishan," "as solid as Mount Taishan," "as weighty as Mount Taishan," and "Mount Taishan and the Big Dipper."

In his late years, when not writing books, Confucius would often stand alone leaning on a walking stick at his doorway, gazing at the distant Mount Taishan. One cold spring morning after getting up, Confucius, in a break from his usual routine, walked outside the house, his hands clasped behind his back and dragging his walking stick, singing to himself: "Mount Taishan is going to break down! The main beam of the house is going to break! The wise man is going to wither and die!" Then, he went back to the house and sat at the door, sighing: "I am probably going to die!"

When his student Zi Gong heard the song, he was filled with foreboding, thinking: "If Mount Taishan is going to break down, where shall I look to with reverence? If the sage is going to die, what teacher, then, shall I follow?"

Seven days later, Confucius passed away, at the age of 73.

Two thousand years on, Emperor Qianlong went to Qufu to hold a memorial service and pay respects to Confucius before his tomb. He seemed to hear the song of Confucius and Zi Gong's apprehension. He wrote: "Your teachings civilized later generations like rains and dew moisten lands; just as great Mount Taishan did not break down, your great image has remained in people's minds."

Indeed! Mount Taishan did not break down, nor did the wise man wither and die away. As the mountain worship ceremonies gradually increased in importance, with every dynasty passed, Confucius was promoted to ever higher noble rank, starting as an educator of humble birth and finishing with the title of "Dacheng Zhisheng Wenxuan Wang (Sage King of Great Achievements in Cultural Dissemination)."

When Confucius was buried, the altar before his tomb was a simple brick and tile platform about two square meters, but by the Han Dynasty, this had become a stone altar. From the Tang Dynasty on, with every mountain worship ceremony on Mount Taishan, emperors would send a sacrificial stone from Mount Taishan and build it into the altar before Confucius' tomb. The symbolism and significance of this action speak volumes.

The nature worship of heaven and earth had since lost any real belief content; of the mountain worship ceremonies, all that was left was fussy forms. Confucius worship, on the other hand, had become the heart of feudal ethics, and the ceremony for offering sacrifices to Confucius had become a national ceremony. His saddle-shaped tomb, though modest in size, replaced the towering Mount Taishan in the hearts of people, becoming ancient China's "saint mountain" that bound together people's minds and society. For over 2,000 years of history, it was the pillar of Chinese society, politics, culture, morality and belief.

The Big Dipper Terrace below the Confucius Cliff was once thought by some to be an ancient observatory. In fact it was a special monument to Confucius. On the summit of Mount Taishan where Confucius "realized the smallness of the empire," the message of Big Dipper Terrace was that Confucius is not only "a sage like Mount Taishan," but also "the Big Dipper around which all stars gather."

Chapter VIII

Rock Inscriptions on Mount Taishan

Why Carve Words in Rocks?

Legend has it that ever since the mythical figure Cang Jie created Chinese characters, the Chinese people believed that characters transmitted magical information, invested with mysterious power allowing them to pass through time and space, carrying an enduring record. Therefore, for a very long time people have been engraving characters onto hard objects.

They chose hard objects for their associations with eternity. Pottery, bronze, iron, bamboo, wood and finally they fixed upon rocks.

Why rocks? The well-known Qing Dynasty scholar and poet Gong Zizhen, disclosed the truth:

Rock does not decay and lives much longer than metal in the universe. It comes in diverse shapes and is hard to move. This is why the ancient people picked rocks and stones instead of metal to carve characters.

Of course, there are three further reasons that Gong Zizhen failed to mention: first, rock comes from nature, and is both plentiful and cheap; second, it is hard but can be worked; third, characters carved on cliffs will live as long as the green hills.

Thus, for people who pursued eternity the idea of inscribing words on the renowned Mount Taishan was an irresistible temptation.

Poem by Emperor Qianlong inscribed on Yufeng (Riding on the Wind) Cliff, as been dubbed the imperial scarlet seal on a natural landscape of Mount Taishan

Wealth of Rock Inscriptions on Mount Taishan

The subject matter of Mount Taishan rock inscriptions includes: royal mountain worship sacrifices; the building and reconstruction of temples; sutra and epitaphs, couplets and poetry in praise of the mountain and the scenery. They fall into two categories, stele and rock, with over 800 of the former and over 1,000 of the latter. Steles are concentrated at the Temple of Mount Taishan, and inscribed rocks are often seen along the central axis and the summit. The stone calligraphy is a feast for the eye, every aspect exhibiting great diversity; in the number and size of characters employed; in the nature of the rock; in the surface preparation and in calligraphic style, from formal to freeform. The calligraphic stones add an air of learning and refinement to the austere, natural Mount Taishan. Abounding in inscribed rocks, commemorative steles and monuments, Mount Taishan has become a natural museum of splendid stone inscriptions and calligraphic art.

Stele and cliffside inscriptions are everywhere on Mount Taishan.

On display in the east corridor of the main hall of the Temple of Mount Taishan are 19 noted steles from every age, of which the most famous are the Eastern Han Dynasty steles to Zhang Qian and to Heng Fang, the Jin Dyansty Stele to Mistress Sun, and the Tang Dynasty Mandarin Ducks Monument.

One corner of the Stele Forest in the Temple of Mount Taishan

Temple of Mount Taishan Inscriptions

Mount Taishan rock calligraphy starts with the Qin Dynasty, to say that it has experienced many ups and downs would be an understatement.

This tablet was engraved in the small seal calligraphic style of Prime Minister Li Si when the First Emperor of Qin made an inspection tour of China's eastern provinces in 219 BC. Ten years later (209 BC), during the reign of the Second Emperor of Qin, the rear side of the tablet was engraved, also in the small seal calligraphic style of Prime Minister Li Si, to announce his imperial edict. There were altogether 222 characters carved on this piece of slightly polished stone. Originally, it stood on the summit, but because it eulogized a tyrant, this tablet, invaluable in terms of the history of China, of Chinese characters and of Chinese calligraphy was hated and, unfortunately, deliberately damaged by people of later times. Over the years, it was damaged both by human beings and natural weathering, including fire and soaking. When retrieved from the Jade Maiden Pond of Bixia Temple in 1851, only two fragmented parts of the original rock bearing ten broken characters were found.

These ten characters constitute a rare treasure, of great significance for the study

Qin Dynasty stone inscription

Stele to Zhang Qian

of the standardization of characters under the Qin Dynasty. Prime Minister Li Si's small seal calligraphic style was solemn and dignified in form, with neat, slim, smooth and gracefully curved lines and a well balanced structure. The First Emperor of Qin stipulated the small seal style as standard throughout China after his uni-

183

fication of the country, so, naturally, Li Si's small seal characters were regarded as the model to be followed.

The tablets at the Temple of Mount Taishan, including those removed there from other places, enjoy great renown in Chinese calligraphic history.

The Stele to Heng Fang was erected in the year 168 during the Eastern Han Dynasty at Guojialou, Wenshang County, and was moved to the Temple of Mount Taishan in 1953. It was engraved in official script. According to the Qing Dynasty calligrapher He Zhaoji, this tablet shows "an unbending manner in simple lines." It helped create the vigorous calligraphic style in Chinese history.

The Stele to Zhang Qian was erected in 186 during the Eastern Han Dynasty. It was excavated in Dong'e County during the Ming Dynasty, and moved to the Temple of Mount Taishan in 1965. From the Ming Dynasty on, calligraphers have been heaping high praise on it; as a masterpiece of Han Dynasty official script calligraphy. This exquisitely carved tablet looks resplendent and varied, with simple yet elegant lines and powerful strokes. The origin of the elegant style in Chinese calligraphy, it established the calligraphic style for the future Wei and Jin dynasties.

The Stele to Heng Fang and the Stele to Zhang Qian are the two of the seven

Stele to Heng Fang

famous extant tablets of the Eastern Han Dynasty, and are regarded as models of Han steles. They attract calligraphy lovers from all parts of the country, as well as Japan and Korea, who often spend a whole day examining them. Though inscribed during the same dynasty, in the same region, and in the same calligraphic style, they are completely different in style, influencing Chinese calligraphy in different ways. Now, they are placed together, allowing detailed comparison, a hugely satisfying artistic experience for visitors.

The Stele to Mistress Sun, one of the three great steles of the Jin Dynasty, was erected in Xintai County in 272. It was moved to the Temple of Mount Taishan in 1965. Written in the current official script style, it combines both the elegance of official script and precision of the regular script, and is regarded by critics as the epitome of Jin Dynasty official script calligraphic style.

The Qizhou Shenbao Temple Stele, a representative work of the official script style of the Tang Dynasty, was carved in 736. The flat and square structure of the characters exhibits a powerful and elegant manner.

The upper part of the Mandarin Ducks Monument is covered with characters of the regular script style. Though they appear not neat, the characters are spontaneous, simple and lovely. Of particular note are the seven inscriptions on the monument, engraved after Wu Zetian proclaimed herself empress of the Tang Dynasty, that include 11 new characters invented by Wu herself.

The Stele Commemorating the Rebuilding of the Temple of Mount Taishan During the Xuanhe Reign was erected during the Xuanhe reign (1119-1125) of the Song Dynasty. Including its turtle base, it stands more than 11 meters high, splendid in its ancient simplicity, and the largest piece at the Temple of Mount Taishan. The smooth and graceful characters remind people of the erudite atmosphere of the Song Dynasty.

The Stele Commemorating the Re-

construction of the Temple of Mount Taishan During the Dading Reign of the Kin Dynasty was erected during the Dading reign period which lasted from 1161 to 1189. The calligraphy, inscriptions and seal characters on the monument were all done by accomplished masters of the day. Hence it gained the accolade "Three-beauty Stele."

Most of the post-Song Dynasty inscriptions at the Temple of Mount Taishan use regular script or running script; few are in cursive hand, too. Together with all the pre-Song Dynasty monuments, they constitute a magnificent treasured classical library of calligraphic art, representing every age. No visitor here, stopping to examine these monuments, can fail to experience a sense of ancient Chinese civilization, and appreciate the Chinese people's adaptability and flexibility of spirit.

The "Three-beauty Stele" recording the renovation of the Temple of Mount Taishan during the Dading Reign of the Kin Dynasty

Two Approaches to Climbing Mountains

A comparison of the different approaches to climbing shown by Chinese people and Westerners reveals two distinct cultural attitudes and tastes.

Westerners love to brave wild, steep high mountains and perilous cliffs, find-ing pleasure in the conquest of nature and danger. This way of climbing exhibits man's strength, knowledge, technique and daring. The Western "martial approach" to climbing was introduced with the Mount Taishan Climbing Festival. It takes less than an hour to run from the Temple of Mount Taishan to Jade Emperor Peak, but this submission of nature

Springtime comes to the summit.

through strength and speed, whilst stirring and exciting, allows no time to enjoy the beautiful scenery en route. It is an approach that stresses objective and result, rather than process and enjoyment; it reminds me of the earthshaking shout in Goethe's *Faust*, "You are so beautiful. Please, linger for a while!"

The way Chinese climb is quite different from that of Westerners; it is a "scholastic approach" displaying a profound attitude toward nature. The Chinese take no shortcuts, deliberately taking the roundabout way so as to take in and enjoy as many views as possible, and when inspiration comes, writing poetry to inscribe upon the cliffs. Gradually, this famous mountain, where so many learned men have trodden and masters of engraving plied their craft, has become covered with stone inscriptions and Mount Taishan has become a splendid book. Mount Taishan's wealth of scenic beauty and stone inscriptions mean that there is only one way to climb the mountain — the Chinese way.

Zhongxi Stream in summer

Autumn at Heavenly Candle Peak

Winter beauty of Bixia Temple

Theme of Stone Inscriptions on Mount Taishan: Ascending

The English historian Goldsworthy Lowes Dickinson, who climbed up Mount Taishan in 1912, regarded it as the holiest mountain in China, and probably the most climbed mountain in the world. Though people of different ages have climbed Mount Taishan with different aims and different levels of understanding, before the building of the winding mountain road and cableway, every single one of them had to go up on foot, step by single step. The excellent poem *Ascending Mount Taishan* written by Abbot Yuanyu of Temple of Omnipresent Light

Inscriptions meaning "Zenith" and "Acme" on the summit

on Mount Taishan in the early Qing Dynasty (1644-1911) describes, "Each step on the ground leads to Heaven; one careless step leaves you far from Heaven; those who come to the very top take every step carefully."

"Ascending to Heaven" was the common theme of all visitors to Mount Taishan from the Emperor down to commoners, so naturally this is the main theme of the cliffside inscriptions.

At the starting point at the foot of the mountain, one at either side of the path, stand two steles carved with words "Number One Mountain" and "You must start here to scale the heights"; these make it clear from the outset that people should proceed step by step with a steadfast spirit, with great concentration and lofty aspirations. The huge Chinese characters meaning "You must start here to scale the heights" in running script calligraphy were engraved in the Ming Dynasty and are a reference to some lines in the Confucian classic *The Doctrine of the Mean*. This plain common sense actually contains profound life philosophy, and can be seen as the first lesson in the textbook of human culture that is Mount Taishan. It was probably so as to further highlight the sacred nature of this spot that it was settled upon as being the place from which Confucius set off to climb Mount Taishan.

Climbing high, like learning from good examples and following the path of virtue, is by no means accomplished in one single leap. Visitors walk north from the Happy Relaxation Path (*kuaihuo sanli*) and, having had a short taste of "Happy Relaxation" on a level path, just as they are faced again with the winding mountain road, an impressive stone inscription appears in their way. The words "Being virtuous is as hard as climbing up a mountain" are a timely reminder to climbers that they have come to a critical point; should they pick up their courage and continue on uphill or feel disheartened and turn back? Remember the proverb left by the Chinese ancestors, "Being virtuous is as hard as climbing up a mountain, but to give in to vice is easy." To achieve a higher level of spiritual and morality has always been like climbing a mountain — the higher you get, the more difficult it becomes and the more effort it requires. In contrast, to indulge one's instinctive desires is like a setting off a landslide in a split second.

By the time they reach Eighteen Mountain Bends most are faint and weak, legs shaking from fatigue. A stone engraved with the plain words "Striving Hard to Climb High" stands by the side of the path. The sentiment was not intended to inspire great feelings but one of intimacy. At this point, it is genial encouragement that is called for, rather than solemn teaching.

Once you get to the top, the Gate to Heaven is clearly in sight and the perilous path of the Stairway to Heaven lies behind and below you. Only then will the feeling of

Inscription at the South Gate to Heaven, Qing Dynasty

"no regret to heaven on high and to other people on earth" rise spontaneously in your heart. You did your best and did not fail heaven; you lived up to your human potential, by advancing steadily and overcoming fear and laziness. Your own efforts have finally brought you to a state of having no regrets at heart and handling dangers without difficulty.

Thousands of steps bring you to the summit of Mount Taishan, and its views of mountains and boundless land spread out below, seas of clouds rolling beneath your feet, and blue sky close enough to touch. The spectacular scenery between heaven and earth is instantly awe-inspiring. Faced with such a spectacle, every one, however wise or dull, noble or humble, will be filled with such lofty emotions and sentiments, as "I am the pinnacle after climbing up a mountain." Each seeks out the stone inscription that best expresses their mood. Each tries to find the inscription most expressive of their feelings and take a picture! Snap! I actually made it to the top of Mount Taishan!

Stone Inscriptions at Cloud Step Bridge

Set by a high waterfall, the Cloud Step Bridge is "a buffer strip" between two long sections of stone steps, and provides a natural rest place for visitors. As a result, it has the highest number of inscriptions — over 50 — of any spot on Mount Taishan.

Mount Taishan owes its fame partly, of course, to the majesty of the mountain itself, but the more important factor is its huge number of inscriptions. The combination of mountain and characters in the inscriptions lends color to the splendor of landscape, which in turn infuses vigor into the inscriptions. Upon seeing them, visitors will be suddenly enlightened and at one with the universe.

"Waterfall at Cloud Bridge," "Cloud Steps Reaching Heaven." "Primary Artery of Mountains and Rivers" are among the 50 plus cliff inscriptions around Cloud Step Bridge.

Waterfall at Cloud Step Bridge

Four Inscriptions of the Same Poem

Many Chinese know the poem *Gazing at Mount Taishan* composed by the Tang poet Du Fu (712-770) as a young man. For over a thousand years, the brilliance of this poem has never been surpassed by any of the nearly ten thousand others on Mount Taishan, and its classic interpretation of the spirit of Mount Taishan has become a clarion call, encouraging people to strive hard and go all out to win success. Almost everyone who climbs Mount Taishan will silently recite its lines at different stages of the ascent. Is it by coincidence or perhaps the communion of hearts that this poem

Du Fu's poem *Gazing at Mount Taishan* written in seal script by Wu Dacheng

appears four times at four different levels on the main route between the Temple of Mount Taishan and the summit?

In the stele corridor of the Temple of Mount Taishan, at the starting of the ascent, stands a stele with the poem inscribed in cursive script by He Renlin, magistrate of Tai'an County during the reign of Emperor Qianlong (1736-1795). Looking up at Mount Taishan in distance arouses precisely the vague feeling described in the poem "How is the view of Mountain Taishan? Its greenness spans all of the Qi and Lu land."

Passing the Ten Thousand Immortal Tower, on the huge stone at the west side of the winding mountain road the poem appears in seal characters by Wu Dacheng, a minister and expert on seal engraving during the reign of Emperor Guangxu (1875-1908). At this spot one savors the artistic mood of the lines "A marvel done by nature's hands, Over light and shade it dominates."

The regular script calligraphy of Tie Bao, governor of Shandong Province and Viceroy of Jiangnan and Jiangxi provinces during the reign of Emperor Jiaqing (1796-1820) is inscribed on the stone directly facing the Eighteen Mountain Bends on the east cliff of the Opposing Pines Mountain. It is a marvelous spot, an embodiment of the words "Clouds rise therefrom and brush my chest; I strain my eyes and see birds returning to the nest."

Finally, on the large stone south of the Immortals Bridge on the summit is the calligraphy in official script of the 20th century scholar Li Yimang. It is exactly the spot place to appreciate the words "I must ascend the mountain's crest, it dwarfs all peaks under my feet."

The four inscriptions happen to reproduce the four perspectives in Du Fu's poem *Gazing at Mount Taishan*. The cursive, regular, seal and official styles of scripts basically cover all the main features of Chinese calligraphy. What a magnificently profound and subtle design to put this poem, the zenith of poetry on Mount Taishan. The four calligraphers, separated by as much as 200 years, had no chance to consult. We cannot but cheer the communion of their hearts.

Du Fu's poem *Gazing at Mount Taishan* inscribed in cursive script by He Renlin

Landscape and Sentiment in Accord

As one would expect, it is inscriptions reflecting the views on Mount Taishan that predominate. Ranging in length from a single character to six, the words, in most cases, are well suited to the landscape, and meanings precisely express the mood, achieving a perfect state of flexibility, refinement and transcendence of spirit.

The following selection of comments made by generations of visitors, the themes divided into pine, rocks, clouds and springs categories, give an overview of the stone inscriptions on Mount Taishan:

Pines: Independent Gentleman, Righteous Noble, Pine in Solitude, Rock for Listening to the Soughing of the Wind in the Pines, Rustling Sound and Cloud Shadow, Pines Gate, and Peaks Covered by Serried Green Pines

Rocks: Tiger, Sword Cutting Clouds, 1000-leaf Stone Lotus Flower, Rock Flying Down, and Old Man Peak

Clouds: In Every Inch Clouds Gather,

The Sister Pines, standing abreast on the Dongyao Viewing Terrace at the Rear Rock Basin, their roots and branches intertwined

"Peaks Covered by Serried Green Pines" describes Opposing Pines Mountain, where two peaks face each other, each luxuriantly clad with myriads of ancient pines.

There was formerly a pine with vigorously sweeping branches on the cliff of the Opposing Pines Mountain. It was named "Independent Gentleman" for its upright posture but was destroyed by a storm several centuries ago; only the inscriptions to it survive, among them, "Independent Gentleman," "Pine Gate," and "Solitary Pine."

Guest Welcoming Pine, its long branches overhanging the winding mountain road, as if bowing to arriving guests

Big and Small Heavenly Candle Peaks, also called Twin Phoenix Ridge, south of Nine-dragon Hill at the Rear Rock Basin. When wind blows, the dense rows of pines move like ocean waves making the "Pine Waves on the Heavenly Candle Peaks" one of the spectacles of Mount Taishan.

Huge column-like rocks sprawl by the Lesser Cave of Immortals near the East Stream behind the Red Gate. In cross-section, the structure of the rock looks like withered trees, with an isotopic age of about 1.1 and 1.3 billion years. The upper rock bears the words "Intoxication of the heart."

The Fan Cliff below Aolai Peak at the West Brook is like a huge towering fan, its sheer pitch giving rise to the name "The Immortal Palm."

Near the Terrace for Viewing Lu, between two sharp cliffs, are three huge rocks that touch to form a natural bridge, named the "Bridge of the Immortals."

Sleeping Cloud, Cloud Gate, Cloud Path, Dancing Clouds, and Heaven Near and Clouds Low

Springs: Vigor of Pines and Beauty of Springs, Purifying Heart and Mind High, Milky Way Falling Down upon Earth, Mountains and Flowing Streams.

In the words of the contemporary aesthetician Zong Baihua: "Chinese people cherish all creatures and share the same life rhythm. We are as quiet and still as *yin* when at rest, as vibrant as *yang* when in motion. Our Universe too has a life rhythm combining *yin* and *yang*, emptiness and substance. Therefore, it is essentially a unity of spirit and soul in space and time and a flowing energy of vibrant tone and flavor."

During a storm in summer 1603, a rock fell from the top of the mountain, landing in front of the Five-gentlemen Pine Stone Arch and was thus called "Rock Flying Over."

Between the sheer peaks of Writing Brush Rest Mountain to the southwest of Peach Blossom Ravine only a thin slat of light can be seen, giving rise to the name "Sliver of Sky."

Among the steep precipices north of Fan Cliff, is a huge rock, shaped like a jade pot and called "Pot Cliff."

That Chinese literati, emperors and princes, generals and ministers of every age should chose the grand and permanent expressive medium of cliffside inscription was obviously related to their grand sense of space and time, as evident in "Heaven and earth coexist with me, and all creatures and I are but one." They seemed to stand at the source of history, overlooking mountains and rivers, above eternal mountains and clouds, their minds thronged with thoughts spanning millennia, able to roam through past and present. People in such a transcendent state seem to hear the gentle voice of the Universe and feel the tolerance of the Creator. It is as if their whole life and spirit were surging out from the confines of oneself, following the soughing wind in the pines, rising high with the clouds and mist, flowing with the streams. By carving out just a few characters into a lifeless stone, they shape it into a kind of spirit. Active thinking extends to infinity as "Everything is there for me, I melt among all everything."

Heaven, earth, mountains, rivers, pines, rocks, clouds, springs ... is not each and every one of these the echo of a great mind and spirit?

The inscription "In Every Inch Clouds Gather" south of Ten Thousand Immortals Tower. The words are taken from the lines "Mists come out when meeting with rock, in every inch clouds gather," in the *Spring and Autumn Annals with Commentaries by Gongyang Gao.*

The inscription reads: "Cloud Stairway Leading to the Gateway to Heaven."

211

"Sea of Clouds" and "Lofty Aspirations" inscriptions at Sun Viewing Peak

"Zenith Peak into Clouds" at the South Gateway to Heaven

Cliffside inscription "Rock Basin in the Clouds" at the Rear Rock Basin

Serried peaks and green trees surround the Triple Step
Cascade situated east of the Palace of Big Dipper Mother.
The rock forms through which the waters of the Flying Dragon
Brook flow have created a stepped cascade.

"Crane Bend," formed by spring water erosion and resembling a magic crane, located
in the Immortal Meeting Valley in the Heavenly Candle Peaks scenic area

From Black Dragon Pool, a waterfall runs down precipitous cliffs directly into a deep pool, called White Dragon Pool, taking its name from the legendary White Dragon, son of the Dragon King of the East Sea, who guarded Mount Taishan from this pool. Emperors of all ages sent key ministers to hold grand rites here to pray for rain. In 1082, the Temple to the Lord of Replenishing Ponds was built here.

North of Black Dragon Pool is an extremely high cliff, with waterfalls like a hanging belt sash, hence its name Heavenly Girdle Spring, meaning the "Girdle of the Son of Heaven."

217

Sutra Rock Valley

After you have gained the satisfaction of "seeing the world dwindle" from the summit of Mount Taishan, be sure not to forget to go to Sutra Rock Valley to dip your feet. In this deep quiet valley, you can hear the steady beating of an age-old heart.

No one can fail to be amazed by the stone inscription here, which covers a surface of 2,000 square meters or more. Carefully studying every stroke on the flat rock imagining that monk more than 1,400 years ago using the rock as paper, wielding a huge, rafter-thick brush, concentrating his mind, radiating with energy and vigor, using the power of body and brush to write with the greatest piety ... who could not be profoundly moved by his dedication and stamina!

The *Diamond Sutra* inscription at Sutra Rock Valley was recently proved to be that of the eminent monk An Daoyi who lived 1,400 years ago. He traveled from the northwest via Henan to the State of Lu, leaving many stone inscriptions of Buddhist scriptures in this homeland of Confucianism. The scale and the calligraphy of those inscriptions are acclaimed as the acme of perfection. An's rock-firm determination and innovative way of promoting Buddhism indeed show his whole-hearted and painstaking efforts.

Why did he engrave the *Diamond Sutra* on Mount Taishan? Was it simply to leave a permanent mark of Buddhism there? Or perhaps An Daoyi, having heard that the souls of Chinese people were gathered at Mount Taishan, thought to cover a whole rock face with texts from the *Diamond Sutra* so as release those souls from suffering and deliver them to the Pure Land? Or perhaps he was aiming a head-on blow to deter any potential imitators of the First Emperor of Qin, and Emperor Wu of Han, who made stupid and conceited attempts to become immortals by performing mountain worship ceremonies at Mount Taishan?

These days we have no way of verifying An Daoyi's true motive any more than we know why the project was dropped halfway. At present, on the enormous stone surface, there are altogether 44 columns of characters from east to west, with between 10 and 125 characters to each column, and over 1,000 characters still preserved.

Sutra Rock Valley used the official script as its main frame, but drew on and absorbed the essence of *Wei* script and seal characters to form a unique style in calligraphic history, namely official-regular script, a style of simple and vigorous, strong and smooth characters. The strokes are well modulated and varied, featuring elongated long strokes and forceful short strokes, stillness and movement complementing each other, and the large gaps between strokes reminiscent of riding a horse on a boundless plateau. Therefore, by reason of its spacious and de-

In 1572, the Ming Dynasty Viceroy of Watercourses Wan Gong built the High Mountains and Flowing Streams Pavilion in Sutra Rock Valley, and wrote travel notes about the pavilion, praising the wonderful combination of mountains, streams and inscriptions. The inscriptions record the building the pavilion.

liberate strokes, this style has gone down in China's calligraphic history as the "ancestor of big characters."

It is a particular point of praise that the sutra texts were actually carved out on what is the widest bed of all the streams on Mount Taishan. Clear waters run over the characters just as river water gradually overflows the shallows. The submerged characters seem like swimming dragons and waving reeds. Water flows over the carved words, splashing, sounding loud and clear like the melody *High Mountains and Flowing Streams.*

Seen from close range the inscribed rocks here look like statues of Buddha, solemn and quiet; from afar they are like cranes flying aloft in the clouds. Set against the background of mountain forest, crags, brooks and sounding bells, the rocks merge into nature and are at one with the universal truths of the Buddhist sutra. Those inscribed stones came into being in the context that "Every creature runs its course in the lonesome eternal universe." In the mystic atmosphere where humans, mountains and rivers co-exist, those stones are the product of transitory lives and ever-lasting mountains. Facing such a magnificent artistic work, one can feel the unseen gaze of the ancients upon us. Both the inscriptions and people, who come to see them, seem to become works of nature. Man seems to find a soul as eternal as the heaven and the hills, and thus experi-

ences a life-affirming joy.

The stone inscriptions on Mount Taishan are the mark of China's contemplative history and of its ancient civilization. These stones are engraved with a dense grain of history and record the aspirations of people through the ages. In their vertical and hori-

zontal strokes are subtly reflected the characteristics of different times and cultures: the harsh rule and law of the Qin Empire bred the strict and neat small seal character; the pioneering, progressive Han culture produced the distinctive and forceful official script; the prosperous and confident Tang Dynasty created the majestic and sumptuous regular script. And the strength and profundity of the Northern Dynasties (386-581) cliffside sutras are a distant reflection of religion's ability to comfort and uplift in troubled times....

Inscriptions of the *Diamond Sutra* in Sutra Rock Valley

Sunrise & Sunset Timetable of Mount Taishan

Date	January		February		March		April		May		June	
	Sunrise	Sunset	Sunrise	Sunset	Sunrise	Sunset	Sunrise	Sunset	Sunrise	Sunset	Sunrise	Sunset
1	7:12	16:53	7:03	17:23	6:34	17:53	5:50	18:20	5:10	18:44	4:46	19:10
2	7:13	16:53	7:02	17:24	6:32	17:53	5:48	18:20	5:08	18:46	4:45	19:10
3	7:13	16:55	7:01	17:25	6:31	17:54	5:47	18:22	5:07	18:47	4:45	19:10
4	7:13	16:56	7:01	17:26	6:30	17:55	5:45	18:22	5:07	18:47	4:44	19:11
5	7:13	16:56	7:00	17:28	6:28	17:56	5:44	18:23	5:05	18:48	4:44	19:12
6	7:13	16:57	6:59	17:28	6:27	17:57	5:42	18:24	5:04	18:49	4:44	19:13
7	7:13	16:58	6:58	17:29	6:26	17:58	5:41	18:25	5:03	18:50	4:44	19:13
8	7:13	16:58	6:57	17:31	6:24	17:59	5:40	18:25	5:02	18:50	4:44	19:14
9	7:13	16:59	6:56	17:31	6:23	18:00	5:38	18:26	5:01	18:52	4:44	19:14
10	7:13	17:01	6:55	17:32	6:21	18:01	5:37	18:27	5:01	18:52	4:43	19:14
11	7:12	17:01	6:55	17:34	6:20	18:02	5:35	18:28	4:59	18:53	4:44	19:15
12	7:12	17:02	6:53	17:35	6:19	18:03	5:34	18:29	4:59	18:54	4:43	19:16
13	7:13	17:03	6:53	17:36	6:17	18:04	5:32	18:30	4:58	18:55	4:43	19:16
14	7:12	17:04	6:52	17:37	6:16	18:04	5:31	18:31	4:57	18:56	4:43	19:17
15	7:12	17:05	6:50	17:38	6:14	18:05	5:30	18:31	4:56	18:57	4:43	9:17
16	7:12	17:06	6:49	17:40	6:13	18:06	5:28	18:32	4:55	18:58	4:43	19:17
17	7:11	17:07	6:49	17:40	6:11	18:07	5:27	18:33	4:55	18:58	4:44	19:17
18	7:11	17:08	6:47	17:41	6:10	18:08	5:25	18:34	4:53	18:59	4:43	19:18
19	7:10	17:09	6:46	17:42	6:08	18:08	5:24	18:35	4:53	19:00	4:43	19:18
20	7:10	17:10	6:44	17:43	6:07	18:10	5:23	18:35	4:52	19:01	4:44	19:19
21	7:10	17:11	6:43	17:44	6:05	18:10	5:22	18:36	4:52	19:01	4:44	19:19
22	7:10	17:12	6:43	17:45	6:04	18:11	5:20	18:37	4:51	19:02	4:44	19:19
23	7:08	17:13	6:41	17:46	6:02	18:12	5:19	18:38	4:50	19:03	4:44	19:19
24	7:08	17:14	6:40	17:47	6:01	18:13	5:18	18:38	4:49	19:04	4:44	19:19
25	7:08	17:15	6:39	17:49	5:59	18:14	5:17	18:40	4:49	19:04	4:45	19:20
26	7:07	17:17	6:37	17:49	5:58	18:15	5:16	18:41	4:48	19:05	4:45	19:20
27	7:07	17:17	6:36	17:50	5:56	18:16	5:14	18:41	4:48	19:06	4:46	19:19
28	7:05	17:19	6:35	17:52	5:55	18:17	5:13	18:42	4:47	19:07	4:46	19:20
29	7:05	17:20			5:54	18:17	5:12	18:43	4:47	19:07	4:46	19:20
30	7:04	17:21			5:53	18:18	5:10	18:44	4:46	19:08	4:46	19:20
31	7:04	17:22			5:51	18:19			4:46	19:08		

Date	July Sunrise	July Sunset	August Sunrise	August Sunset	September Sunrise	September Sunset	October Sunrise	October Sunset	November Sunrise	November Sunset	December Sunrise	December Sunset
1	4:47	19:20	5:08	19:05	5:32	18:29	5:55	17:44	6:23	17:04	6:54	16:44
2	4:47	19:20	5:08	19:05	5:34	18:28	5:56	17:43	6:25	17:03	6:55	16:44
3	4:48	19:19	5:09	19:04	5:34	18:26	5:57	17:41	6:25	17:02	6:55	16:44
4	4:49	19:20	5:10	19:03	5:34	18:25	5:58	17:40	6:26	17:01	6:56	16:44
5	4:49	19:19	5:11	19:02	5:35	18:23	5:59	17:38	6:28	17:00	6:57	16:44
6	4:49	19:19	5:11	19:01	5:36	18:22	5:59	17:37	6:28	16:59	6:58	16:44
7	4:50	19:19	5:12	19:00	5:37	18:20	6:00	17:36	6:29	16:58	6:59	16:43
8	4:50	19:19	5:13	18:59	5:38	18:19	6:01	17:34	6:31	16:57	6:59	16:44
9	4:51	19:19	5:14	18:58	5:38	18:17	6:02	17:33	6:31	16:56	7:01	16:44
10	4:52	19:18	5:15	18:57	5:39	18:16	6:02	17:31	6:32	16:55	7:02	16:44
11	4:52	19:19	5:16	18:55	5:40	18:14	6:04	17:30	6:34	16:55	7:02	16:44
12	4:53	19:18	5:16	18:55	5:41	18:13	6:04	17:28	6:35	16:54	7:03	16:44
13	4:53	19:17	5:17	18:53	5:41	18:11	6:05	17:27	6:35	16:53	7:04	16:44
14	4:54	19:17	5:18	18:53	5:42	18:10	6:07	17:26	6:37	16:52	7:04	16:44
15	4:55	19:17	5:19	18:51	5:43	18:08	6:07	17:25	6:38	16:52	7:05	16:44
16	4:56	19:16	5:20	18:50	5:44	18:07	6:08	17:23	6:39	16:51	7:05	16:45
17	4:56	19:16	5:20	18:49	5:44	18:05	6:09	17:22	6:40	16:50	7:06	16:46
18	4:57	19:15	5:21	18:47	5:45	18:04	6:10	17:20	6:40	16:50	7:07	16:45
19	4:58	19:14	5:22	18:46	5:46	18:02	6:11	17:19	6:42	16:49	7:07	16:46
20	4:58	19:14	5:23	18:46	5:47	18:01	6:12	17:18	6:43	16:49	7:08	16:46
21	4:59	19:14	5:23	18:44	5:47	17:59	6:13	17:16	6:44	16:49	7:08	16:47
22	5:00	19:13	5:25	18:43	5:48	17:58	6:13	17:16	6:45	16:47	7:08	16:47
23	5:01	19:13	5:25	18:41	5:49	17:56	6:14	17:14	6:46	16:47	7:09	16:47
24	5:01	19:12	5:26	18:40	5:50	17:55	6:16	17:13	6:47	16:47	7:10	16:48
25	5:02	19:11	5:27	18:39	5:51	17:53	6:16	17:11	6:47	16:46	7:10	16:49
26	5:03	19:10	5:28	18:37	5:52	17:52	6:17	17:10	6:49	16:46	7:11	16:49
27	5:04	19:10	5:29	18:36	5:52	17:50	6:18	17:10	6:50	16:45	7:11	16:49
28	5:04	19:09	5:29	18:34	5:53	17:49	6:19	17:08	6:51	16:45	7:11	16:50
29	5:05	19:08	5:30	18:34	5:53	17:47	6:20	17:07	6:52	16:45	7:11	16:51
30	5:06	19:07	5:31	18:32	5:55	17:46	6:22	17:06	6:53	16:44	7:12	16:52
31	5:07	19:07	5:32	18:31			6:22	17:05			7:12	16:52

Monthly Average Temperature of Mount Taishan (centigrade)

Month	Foot of Taishan	Top of Taishan
1	-2	-7.8
2	0.6	-6.3
3	6.6	-1.3
4	14	6
5	19.3	11.6
6	24.5	15.8
7	26.2	17.9
8	25.2	17.1
9	20.4	12.7
10	14.2	7.2
11	6.4	0.2
12	0.1	-5.4

Best Time to Visit Mount Taishan

The best times to visit Mount Taishan are: first, around the May Day Holiday, when spring is at its peak, peach trees are in bloom, and nature returns to life after harsh winter; second, in midsummer, when Mount Taishan is a vivid picture of cliffside springs and cascading waterfalls, lush pines, a riot of flowers, and bird song; third, in autumn around the 1st October when days are fine and the skies clear, when fruits and flowers fill the valleys, and the peaks are tinged with autumn gold; and fourth, in the depth of winter, on fine days when translucent ice blooms glitter in the sunshine, with the wind soughing, and during heavy snows, with the mountain "dancing like a silver serpent" — a quintessential north country scene.

Ranking of Hotels in Tai'an

Name of Hotel	Location	Telephone	Stars
Taishan Huaqiao Hotel	15 Dongyue Street	0538-8228112	★★★★
Taishan Hotel, Tai'an	26 Hongmen Road	0538-8224678	★★★
Jinshan Holiday Village	137 Huanshan Road	0538-8225254	★★★
Tai'an Yuzuo Hotel	50 North Daimiao Road	0538-8269999	★★★
Shenqi Hotel (top of the mountain)	10 Heavenly Street n on top of Taishan	0538-8223866	★★★
Shenqi Hotel (foot of the mountain)	158 Tiger Hill Road	0538-8337025	★★★
Taishan Grand Hotel	210 Daizong Street	0538-8227211	★★★
Oriental Holiday Hotel	32 Dongyue Street	0538-8295066	★★★
Oriental Hotel	65 Dragon Pool Road	0538-6223276	★★★
Golden Sea Hotel	96 Yingxuan Street	0538-8228899	★★★
Hongqiao Hotel	West Dongyue Street	0538-8412111	★★★
Friendship Hotel	49 Dongyue Street	0538-8222288	★★★
Dongdu Hotel	279 Daizhong Street	0538-8227948	★★★
Yaochi Hotel	North of Tiger Hill East Road	0538-8211728	★★★
Xindu Hotel	43 Dongyue Street	0538-8227813	★★★
Puzhao Hotel	East, Leigushi Street	0538-8226869	★★★
Huatai Hotel	Central Yingsheng Road	0538-2105857	★★★
Taishan Hotel	123 Daizong Street	0538-6361033	★★★

图书在版编目（CIP）数据

中华第一山: 泰山 / 孙承志主编.
北京: 外文出版社, 2005 (全景中国)
ISBN 7-119-04176-2
I. 中... II. 孙... III. 泰山—简介—英文 IV.K928.3
中国版本图书馆CIP数据核字（2005）第 084642 号

全景中国—山东：中华第一山——泰山

主　　编：孙承志
执行主编：杜广华
撰　　稿：王鲁湘
特约审稿：汤贵仁
图片简介：李继生
编　　辑：李继生 李　静 范宝品
图片提供：(以姓氏笔划为序)
　　　　　亓顺民 孔红宴 王树寅 丛树敏 孙永学 孙立华 闫　实 宋其忠 宋建伟
　　　　　张广坪 张仁东 张健骐 张登山 时盘棋 李怀仁 李　明 陈　勇 范宝品
　　　　　姚群生 思　雨 袁明英 常一诺 晨　曦 解九江 翟　健 魏　武

编　　审：廖　频
责任编辑：刘承忠
装帧设计：蔡　荣
印刷监制：韩少乙

© 2006　外文出版社
出版发行：
外文出版社（中国北京百万庄大街 24 号）
邮政编码 100037　http://www.flp.com.cn
制　　版：
外文出版社照排中心
印　　制：
北京京都六环印刷厂

开本：980mm × 710mm 1/16（平装）印张：15.50
2006 年第 1 版第 2 次印刷
（英）
ISBN 7-119-04176-2
09800
85-E-582P